Change – Becoming a Confident and Bold Leader

26 Articles on Empowering Leadership, Culture, and Strategy

Written by Paul R. Fournier

Company capacity is determined by its leadership capacity.

—Paul R. Fournier

Copyright ©2024 by Paul R. Fournier

All rights reserved. No part of this publication may be reproduced in any manner without written permission of Fournier Books.

For permission requests please contact Paul Fournier at Fournier Books at:

Fournier Books
PO Box 15386
Lenexa KS, 66285 USA
Email: pfournier@fournierbooks.com

	Page Reference
Table of Contents	
Preface	3
Concepts in Confident and Bold Leadership	8
Article 1 - Leadership is the Bedrock of Successful Business	12
Article 2 - Leadership - Five Qualities for Success	17
Article 3 - Growing Brand Equity	24
Article 4 - Creating Positive Change in Your Organization	28
Article 5 - Finding Greater Potential	32
Article 6 - Critical Thinking, Managing Through Chaos	38
Article 7 - Fewer Teachable Moments	44
Article 8 - Pulling Back the Curtain for Growth	49
Article 9 - Reimagine your Organizational Quality	52
Concepts about Customers, Revenue, and Relationships	55
Article 10 - Customer Relevance, How Relevant is your Business	58
Article 11 - Customer Loyalty	63
Article 12 - Sales Revenue Growth, Becoming Customer Centric	70

Article 13 - Financial Capacity: The Impact of Company Culture on the Financial Statement	77
Article 14 - Customer Relationships, Do We know or Assume our Customer Relationships	92
Article 15 - Customer Perspective, Improving Organizational Quality	99

Concepts about Culture Management and Organizational Structure — 105

Article 16 - Organizational Quality	108
Article 17 - What is a Business System	111
Article 18 - Embracing Cultural Health	116
Article 19 - Improving Challenged Cultures, Cultural Management Systems	120
Article 20 - Shareholder Value, It's About People	132
Article 21 - Disruptors to Sales Revenue, The Impact of Leadership and Culture Management	139
Article 22 - Culture Management, What We Don't Know Does Hurt Us	144
Article 23 - Company Health Goes Beyond EBITA	149
Article 24 - Revolutionize Your Culture	153
Article 25 - Selecting Quality Employees	163
Article 26 - Boiled Business (Frog) Syndrome	169

Summary — 178

Preface

I have always been fascinated by honeybees[1]. They are critical to the pollination of flowers, vegetables, and production of honey. They also reflect humanity and resemble simplicity in business structure.

Did You Know

Honeybees[2] are highly organized. They have three adult castes[3]: queen, workers, and drones. Queens lay eggs. Female workers collect pollen. Drones mate with the queen so she can produce thousands of eggs.

Hives can contain 20,000 to 80,000 workers. Workers can travel 2-3 miles or more to collect nectar, pollen, and water.

Queens can live for 3-4 years. Worker bees live for 5-6 weeks. Drones survive a few weeks depending on their mating success.

Queens excrete pheromones or chemical signals which manage the behavior of the hive. Angry hives which can swarm and attack people, seem to have angry queens with angry pheromones. Friendly hives seem to have friendly queens which beekeepers handle without protection.

Beekeepers have learned they can sometimes change hive behavior by transplanting and replacing the old queen with a gentler queen. After 4-6 weeks with a new queen, the hive becomes less aggressive.

---

[1] The Feminin' Monarchi
[2] The British Beekeepers Association
[3] Orkin

Change In a Beehive

Change happens in the beehive with the beekeepers patience and a plan. Rather than extermination, the existing hive survives with new leadership and behaviors.

In business, leadership, employee behaviors, and organizational quality is much the same. We need to plan for change.

The Smell of Solutions

My hardware store has a particular smell. It's the smell of solutions. Interestingly, it's been in the same location for over 60 years stocking almost anything you can imagine.

Wood, plumbing, electrical, tools, garden, pest control, and every gadget known to man is in there. Each contribute to the smell of solutions.

The main aisle of the store has a giant fan. It's slightly slanted to one side of the aisle so one can pass by. The fan runs constantly nine months of the year.

There's a moderate vibrating rumble as you approach. Then, cool air rushes by at head level. Whatever sweat and frustration is on your brow is blown off and replaced with sense of calm.

On a warm day one can stand in front of the fan appreciating the cool for a few minutes. No one from the store ever bothers you as it's a sacred spot. As the air blows by, the worries of the day suddenly leave you. In only a few moments, one has a different prospective of everything.

The sounds and breeze of the fan is deceiving. Not only does it furnish both a cool breeze and comfort, but it communicates predictability and trust.

Trust that if I purchase the wrong item, I can return it. Trust that someone with more experience can guide me to the proper item. Trust that someone can tell me how to install it.

The magic words the fan communicates are predictability and trust. The fan is a form of communication. While you can smell the solutions in the hardware store, but as you leave the taste the success of solving a challenge.

Becoming a Confident and Bold Leader is first about communication. Commerce is the flow of goods, services, and value from one party to another. Secondly, it's about how the relationship contributes to the leadership, culture, and strategy.

The process of how owners, executives, and managers communicate to employees, customers, and suppliers determines the quality of the organization. The quality of communication determines its revenue and earnings.

Success is not a given. Abraham Lincoln[4] failed 67 times in his career before being elected as president of the United States.

The fact is everyone fails at some point in their life. If they haven't, time still awaits. Or your goals are parochial. Failure comes in many forms. Personal, family, or business failures are the most obvious for this discussion.

---

[4] Abraham Lincoln

Sometimes there are reasons and solutions. Other times there are reasons and no solutions.

What's so interesting about failure is the collateral damage inflicted on others. It's the perception we establish with others in the act of failure that separates leaders from the crowd.

In business, collateral damage comes in the form of terminations, layoffs, and financial distress. Business failures generally occur because of the absence of leadership, culture, and effective strategies.

Family failure comes in the form of divorce, challenges of children, financial, or the insecurities of a partner. Each attribute contributes to the notion of failure.

Personal failure comes in the form of career stagnation, termination, or failure to complete objectives. Sometimes its personal behaviors and vices that are contributing factors.

Job entitlement and privilege is a temporary illusion in business. We all experience the same routines each morning and night. As history has proven, we can fall from grace rather quickly when expectations and performance requirements are absent.

Advanced education without rudimentary judgement creates a similar scenario. Real life has greater expectations.

Life isn't fair. Life can be rather cruel. Unfortunately for some, just when the stars align and all the hard tasks are completed, reality of failure rears its ugly head and strikes. Sometimes the venom is paralyzing. Other times it is a gift.

Successful managers create successful environments. They base decisions on honor, integrity, and experience. Poorly conceived goals and relationships seldom improve over time.

Life is an equal balance of personal, family, and business achievements. Each complements the other. When one is performing poorly, most likely the others are struggling as well.

Surviving failure makes us stronger and more resilient. It teaches us hard lesson if we listen. It facilitates the growth of our values and honor.

Becoming a Confident and Bold Leader is about perspective. Does the organization consistently demonstrate Bold Behaviors or Chaos Management?

People are complicated. Facilities and machines are tangible. Equipment has a maintenance timetable for repairs. Employees on the other hand, have multiple conditions and challenges.

Humans are imperfect. There is seldom a perfect solution. But one condition is clear. People want to be led, not driven. That is leadership.

Section 1
Concepts in Confident and Bold Leadership

Change – Becoming a Confident and Bold Leader is a series of 26 articles focused on leadership, culture, strategy, and communication. Each article is a contributor to the cornerstones of successful business.

What drives Confident and Bold Leaders? Why are Confident and Bold Leaders more successful? Each article shares perspective how **effective** leaders better harness the skills, talents, and performance of their team.

Simply, Confident and Bold Leaders communicate goals and strategies effectively. They are decisive, establish equal accountability, and performance expectations that are realistic and fair.

My articles are based on experience and observation. They are designed to probe your critical thinking and perspective.

I have categorized my articles into 3 actionable groups.

- Articles about Leadership
- Articles about Customers, Revenue, and Relationships
- Articles about Culture Management and Organizational Structure

Leadership and strategy provide the plan, course, and speed of the organization. Culture contributes to quality, service, and value. Communication is the glue uniting management, employees, and customers.

Consider this, sales revenue is a result. Profitability is a result. Employee retention is a result. Customer loyalty is a result. Innovation is a result.

Each are a result of the combined power of effective leadership, culture, and strategy. The fact is confident and bold leaders are simply more effective.

Article 1

Leadership is the Bedrock of Successful Business

I engage with organizations from a variety of industries. When we meet, management shares their vision and challenges. Invariably, their challenges generally lead to three common conditions. They are,

1. Unpredictable sales revenue
2. Failure to achieve objectives
3. Profitability

What is interesting is that these conditions are symptoms, not a source. Symptoms mask the source. When management solves for the symptoms, they also create dysfunction and chaos.

> *Most companies solve for symptoms, not the source of challenges.*

History tends to repeat itself. Often these same repetitive conditions occur over years with the same repetitive approaches by management. A cycle is established.

The reality is customers, employees, suppliers, and shareholders expect 100%. In the end, brands improve or become irrelevant.

Bedrock and Leadership

We've all watched the demise of buildings slowly sliding down hills because they were not anchored to bedrock.

Leadership is the bedrock of a successful business. All other components of the business foundation is anchored to the bedrock of leadership. Successful companies realize leadership is a critical and evolving role.

Management from C-suite to line management are facilitators. They,

- Facilitate the success of their organization and teams
- Provide consistent guidance
- Are stewards of their culture
- Identify opportunities, then develop strategies to achieve them
- Hold employees equally accountable

Without effective leadership, culture is vague and assumed. Without a healthy culture there is inconsistent strategy and achievement. Dysfunction and chaos management is routine.

#1- Unpredictable Sales Revenue

Customer attrition is the greatest contributor to unpredictable sales revenue growth. Even the world's greatest salesperson can't sell poor quality, service, and value for long.

Customers expect quality, service, and value to be 100% compliant. They expect innovation and new value creation from suppliers.

Customer attrition is often self-inflicted. And generally, it's not about price, it's about business practices. That's where inconsistent quality, service, and value implodes the customer relationship.

Customer satisfaction is transactional. Every satisfied customer order does matter.

Consider this real time example. Management tasks sales with an annual growth number of 6%. Additionally, the company is experiencing a customer attrition rate of 5%.

Sales is responsible for overcoming the attrition percentage rate plus the sales growth rate. So, if the expected growth rate is 6% and the customer attrition rate is 5%. The true sales objective is 11%.

11% sales revenue growth is difficult to achieve in a challenged economy. And these conditions make it even more difficult to gain competitive advantage. If management had satisfied customer expectations, the attrition rate would be a moderate 2-3 percent.

Sure, every sales teams need professional sales training along with product knowledge and applications. But when poor business practices fails customer expectations, companies set the stage for unpredictable sales revenue.

#2- Failure to Achieve Objectives

Who is at fault when the organization fails to achieve its objectives? Is the burden of responsibility on employees or management? In my experience its generally managements responsibility.

The old acronym of SMART objectives comes to mind. That is SMART (strategic, measured, actionable, realistic, timely). The concept is timeless.

I'm witness to many objectives that are not SMART. They are not SMART because the initial goal and strategy were flawed. SMART objectives then pursue a defective goal and strategy.

Poorly designed strategies plague even the largest companies. Larger companies generally have the financial resources to overcome or recover from poor decisions. Smaller companies do not have the luxury of financial resources to recover from poor decisions.

Most company planning is focused on how to do something, rather than should they be doing it at all.

Flying blind, assumption, or management by the seat of one pants is probably more accurate in describing dysfunctional strategic planning. In this case strategic planning is often focused on how to achieve a goal. Rather than, through careful vetting, should the company pursue and invest its resources in a more realistic goal and strategy.

Organizations utilizing a strategic planning model are more likely to make better strategy decisions. The level of success is parallel to the effectiveness of the plan. By doing so, more objectives are achieved.

#3- Profitability

Profit allows business to exist. Without profit, business ceases or struggles to exist. Without profit, innovation ceases.

There is a balance between product or service price and the customers expectation of what the price should be. Undervalued, the company and its employees become a commodity. Overvalued, sales stall.

Consider this, suppliers gain maximum profit margins when they are consistently delivering quality, service and value. Reality is quality; customers understand there is increased operational costs associated with operating a high-quality business.

What costs the customer more, a higher price, or flawed quality, service and value from their last order?

While competitors may offer lower prices, are they delivering total value? Quality organizations have learned through customer satisfaction scores they gain competitive advantage by delivering quality at 100% all the time.

Concepts to Ponder

1. Does your organization both measure and respond to key performance indicators (KPI's) regarding customer satisfaction?
2. Does your organization solve symptoms or the source of its challenges?
3. How effective is the organization in completing its strategic objectives?

Article 2

Leadership- Five Qualities for Success

What is Leadership?

Today's workforce is more diverse, educated, and informed than ever before. They understand the notion of effective leadership. They expect a quality work environment, TEAM, fair accountability and compensation.

> *Merriam-Webster defines leadership "as the ability to guide, direct, or influence people."*

We see all kinds of leaders. Some are more successful than others. Some have a transformational approach, while others demonstrate a more dictatorial style.

Leadership is a balance. A leader requires the respect of others to be considered a leader. Leaders are not entitled to respect, it's earned.

Leaders establish perception. Leadership styles which are constantly changing send mixed messages. Leadership isn't about extremes, it's about consistency.

Sometimes people confuse leadership with education. Education provides one with more tools and perspective, not necessarily judgment or leadership skills.

The recipe for leadership is consistent simplicity. These five attributes offer a solid foundation for quality leadership.

Value Statements

Leaders who consistently follow company mission, vision, and core values send a message of predictable behavior to employees and customers. When employees and customers observe leaders straying from the mission, vision, and core values they develop doubt and become skeptical.

Too many skeptics invite scrutiny and cultural shifts within the company. These cultural shifts are transmitted to customers, suppliers, and competitors.

Experienced team members begin to question the leadership skills of the individual and management team. This hampers the ability of the company to achieve its strategy and objectives.

Challenges to core values eventually cascade down to every level of the company. We usually observe it in the form of productivity losses, employee turnover, and diminished sales revenue.

Companies pursuing new innovation and opportunities allow enterprises to grow and expand. Wise leaders incorporate value statements and consistent processes into every new opportunity. This communicates one message to gain commitment and positive perception.

Tip: Are your mission, vision, and core values on task? Do they reflect stakeholder goals? Does the leadership team align to these values?

Listening

Effective leaders are great listeners. They seek to understand so they can assess and guide. Leaders should encourage others to share in a constructive process. Listening invites collaboration and commitment which supports a strong culture.

Leaders making impulsive decisions built on emotion, speculation, and inaccurate facts sometimes lead entire organizations astray. Effective leaders who gather facts and opinions from others tend to make more informed decisions.

People want to contribute and be heard. Subordinates want to be included in the contribution process and success of the organization. Leaders advocating listening develop a more strategic enterprise.

It's difficult to operate a quality enterprise without TEAM. Leaders need the support and advice of others. Creating an environment where "Listening" is viewed as an important process develops confidence and self-management among the team.

Tip: Do you actively listen to what others communicate? Is the environment such that others have the opportunity to express their views. Are you approachable and respectful of others input?

Risk

Quality leaders don't put enterprises or employees at excessive risk. Leaders should assess risk on a constant basis understanding there is always some level of market risk. Leaders don't bet on maybe's. They plan for a predictable outcome.

People by nature are not risk-takers. Leaders tend to be greater risk-takers. When a leader makes decisions threatening business perpetuity, or job loss, people become wary and threatened.

When the organization's intellectual capital begins to question leadership skills, perception diminishes. While change is inevitable, excessive risk can damage the respect of both employees and customers.

Customers become dubious of suppliers with ineffective leaders. When quality products, supply chain, and service are interrupted, customers seek other suppliers. Quality customers have a very limited tolerance for dysfunction.

Leadership not understanding the boundaries or constraints of internal initiatives and projects is a source of risk. A very relevant example we've seen is the installation/application of ERP systems (Enterprise Resource Planning). Leaders not understanding the expectations and requirements of the system create dysfunction.

Effective planning is a process to mitigate risk. Enterprises with well-defined strategies and operating plans tend to establish a risk threshold. That is, they decide what acceptable risk is, and what is not. Included in this risk threshold is customer satisfaction.

Leaders, who leap first and later try to figure out solutions, send a clear message to subordinates and customers about their leadership skills.

Tip: Do you operate with a defined risk threshold? Is information management and strategic planning part of the operating environment?

Fair Accountability

Fair accountability is a concept stating,

Management and employees should be held to fair and equal standards.

We have conducted a significant number of 360° Organizational Assessments. One of the most common challenges to leadership from the employees view is *unequal accountability*.

Leadership as I noted earlier, "is ability to guide, direct, or influence people." Without well-defined expectations, a leader is communicating they lack consistent standards. The performance bar is often vague and sometimes misunderstood. How does a leader effectively influence others when clear expectations are absent?

Leaders are responsible for their actions and behaviors. Not every initiative or strategy is going to be perfect. When something is not right take responsibility, then dig in to succeed.

Legacy relationships tend to cloud the practice of fair accountability. Tenured employees with less than acceptable performance or habits cannot be overlooked.

Effective leaders understand tenure is not an entitlement for performance.

All people have some form of challenge. Some have no solutions. Leadership has a human component if you want to sleep at night.

The human component of leadership should have a moderate level of empathy for those with personal and career challenges. Those with challenges should have an action plan with a completion date to correct deficiencies.

Tip: Do performance standards and fair accountability exist in the company? Do all managers subscribe to professional business practices and communication? Has an Employee Assessment been completed to measure success?

Culture

Culture is everything. Culture defines the human capital of the organization. It's the bedrock for sales revenue and earnings. Continuous people improvement sparks critical thinking and innovation. Employee perception translates into customer perception and satisfaction.

Leaders developing a positive culture can feel it. Take the time to really observe an employee work area or production plant. Observe the behavior of management and employee's.

If employees are smiling, productive, and engaged, chances are your culture is on the right track. If it's a sweatshop and activity based, maybe it's time to understand why.

Effective leaders measure and manage the pulse of their company culture. They never assume it's perfect. Cultures change as companies grow. Subcultures develop and it's important for leaders to recognize the boundaries of these cultures.

Tip: What is the status of your company culture? Has it been assessed? Do people better respect leadership or threat?

Concepts to Ponder

1. Do all management team members adhere to the vision, mission and core values of the organization?
2. What is the employee attrition rate?
3. Does the organization measure culture through assessment?

Article 3

Growing Brand Equity

I suggest that leadership, company culture, and effective strategies are the primary source of growing Brand Equity.

The proverbial Silver Bullet for people-related challenges simply does not exist. Every customer transaction is impacted by the quality of the organization. But keep in mind our dialogue is not about basic business mechanics; it's about communication and the quality of both our customers and employees.

Brand Equity

Brand equity is defined as follows:

When a company has positive brand equity, customers invite collaboration and innovation, trust delivers competitive advantage, and shareholder value is maximized.

Brand equity is defined by the total quality of the organization. Total quality rests on a foundation of Leadership, Culture, and Strategy. As we strive to increase the value of Brand Equity, management's assessment of perception changes.

Without clear and effective leadership, culture has few boundaries or expectations. Without a quality culture, strategy is poorly executed or tactical in nature. All is dependent on the quality of the leadership team.

Customers, employees, managers and suppliers all contribute to brand equity. Each contribute to the success of the organization. All departments contribute to brand equity.

Financially, brand equity is measured by the (Value of All Assets – (minus) the Value of All Liabilities. As sales revenue grows through best practices, liabilities generally diminish as a percentage.

Pivot Your Thinking

Relationships are transactional. That is, company relationships with customers, employees, and suppliers are modified with each personal interaction, communication, or order transaction.

Relationship quality is determined by the level of trust between both parties. Brand equity growth begins with understanding the value of trust.

> *"Trust is defined as - assured reliance on the character, ability, strength, or truth of someone or something."* — *Merriam-Webster*

Customers failing to trust a supplier limit their exposure. First, they limit order dependence. Secondly, they seek out alternative suppliers to mitigate risk.

Third, because they lack trust, they fail to collaborate and innovate with the supplier. Frankly, it's a predictable response to trust challenges. The result, sales revenue stagnates, and brand equity diminishes.

Employees failing to trust the company simply look for other employment. Employee attrition rates escalate when management creates an environment of hostility, or unequal job accountability. Job performance declines as does quality communication with customers. The result, sales revenue stagnates, and brand equity diminishes.

Suppliers failing to trust the company limit their financial risk. They see the customers "House of Cards" floundering under the weight of challenged leadership.

Suppliers have the right to choose and invest in their customers. When the company-supplier relationship is challenged, suppliers view the company as a risk, and they quickly move on to better pastures.

Disruptors of Brand Equity

Effective leaders consistently verify the cultural health of the organization. Without a healthy management approach, employee culture, performance, and relationships erode.

Disruption to brand equity growth occurs when these conditions are not top of mind by leadership.

1. Quality: products/service exactly as promised
2. Relationships: consistent and professional relationships
3. Retention: of customers, employees, managers, and suppliers
4. Service: timely, actionable, and friendly solutions resolving challenges
5. Innovation: true innovation that contributes to growth
6. Value: fair and predictable pricing

Downstream Consequences

Companies embracing healthy leadership, culture, and effective strategies live differently. They have a collaborative relationship with customers, employees, and suppliers. The difference is communication, accountability, and achievement. All parties are striving for excellence.

Without effective leadership, culture and strategy wander. Brand equity struggles to meet its potential. The business fails to retain or gain competitive advantage. The business ceases to be relevant.

What's My Culture?

Bench-marking your company culture is the first step in increasing brand equity. The 360° Organizational Assessment identifies areas of opportunity.

The assessment is an excellent indicator of why Brand Equity could be challenged in your organization.

After one understands cultural key indicators, plans can be made for improvement. Cultural change is not a quick fix. It requires commitment, engagement, and accountability

Concepts to Ponder

1. Is Brand Equity increasing within your organization?
2. Is innovation a key component of the organizations revenue stream?
3. Do employees and customers trust the organization to always do the right thing?

Article 4
Creating Positive Change in Your Organization

Planned change is a good thing. Planned change keeps the business relevant. Relevant to both customer and employee perception. Planned change communicates management is pursuing improvements to the organization. Effective and actionable change management reflects the quality of leadership, culture, and strategy.

Reactive change generally means existing conditions changed and management was unprepared. New conditions forced management to react. The result is customers see potential challenges to their orders. Employees see reactive change as a threat to their well-being.

Complacency has consequences. Those consequences sometimes keep organizations from being or remaining a preferred supplier. Complacency also impacts organizations in terms of product quality, service, and value.

Fear Factor

Fear is a basic human emotion. The level of fear is determined by the amount of risk. High risk, and the fear factor multiples for management and employees. Low risk and fear is manageable.

Employees generally fear change. And for good reason. First, they fear change because it might threaten their job and livelihood. Secondly, change often translates into dysfunction and chaos in the work environment when poorly planned.

Customers fear change because it might impact on their orders and supply chain. The customer may be forced to source their needs from other suppliers. Customer buyers have learned in this environment to source other suppliers and anticipate risk.

Good or Bad, Change Influences Customer Perception

Any change influences customer perception. Trust is the operational word. When customer scrutiny is negative, we invite competitors to the party. When the customer cannot depend on the supplier for their orders, they seek the security of predictable supply.

What is your organizations customer perception? The following are several key contributors to customer perception.

- Is your organization viewed as proactive, reactive, or inactive?
- Is quality and service predictable?
- Is innovation effective?
- Does the team communicate effectively and deliver value?
- What is the customer retention rate?

Good or Bad, Change Invites Employee Scrutiny

What history does your organization have regarding operational change? Is it coordinated and well planned, or reactive and dysfunctional? Employee perception establishes the quality of the culture.

- Is management viewed as proactive, reactive, or inactive?
- Does the organization support a healthy culture?
- Is quality, service, and value a key performance indicator?
- Is the organization objective or task driven?
- What is the employee retention rate?

Communication

Quality communication is a tremendous contributor to perception. Companies communicating a well-constructed message about change and improvements builds trust.

Positive trust is built on predictability. Quality communication signals management is challenging their organization to improve.

When customers and employees understand the why and how, they generally take a positive view. And when conditions go off course, they trust management is working to repair the dysfunction.

Transparency

There are few secrets in most organizations. Employees are quick to recognize transparency, or the lack thereof.

Customers are quick to see dysfunction in quality, service, and value. The following are three suggestions for management.

1. Assess and prioritize the organization for barriers to customer satisfaction.
2. Assess and prioritize the organization for barriers to employee culture.
3. Strategize and develop a proactive plan for improvement.

Concepts to Ponder

1. What is the employee fear factor level in the organization?
2. Is change in the organization generally planned or reactive?
3. Is management relevant to customer expectations?

Article 5

Finding Greater Potential

Entrepreneurs generally have a grand vision. Typically, the vision begins on the back of a napkin, between dreams in the middle of the night, or over a beverage with like-minded friends. Suddenly, the vision explodes into a brand.

The magic of the brand evolves into a small organization. Managers, employees, and even customers contribute to shaping the brand.

Sales grow, products or services increase, and the company expands its footprint. The small organization becomes a medium-sized organization with many employees and customers.

Employees establish feelings about the company and its management. These feelings establish perception and form a cultural environment. The cultural environment communicates a relationship and level of quality to every customer with each transaction.

Customer loyalty is built on the success of each transaction. Healthy cultures greatly contribute to the value of customer relationships. In fact, they contribute to competitive advantage.

Until it Doesn't

Entrepreneurial spirit drives the organization until it doesn't. Entrepreneurial spirit is slowly negated by daily challenges and structural deficiencies as the business grows. Incredible effort and long hours by management maintains the organization but fails to significantly grow the organization.

The business has exceeded the capacity of the management team. This is the time where finding greater potential begins with valuing and embracing business systems in management, culture, and strategy

Leadership

Leadership and management do not share like job definitions. Leaders are stewards of the organization, its employees, and products. They facilitate and enforce the vision statement and core values.

Effective managers, on the other hand, are focused on the mission. They achieve objectives by facilitating the efforts of employees. They work within the boundaries of the mission and company core values. Effective managers are instrumental in deploying their organizational skills and execution.

Not everyone can be a great visionary. Highly effective managers are sometimes not outstanding visionaries. Sometimes leaders are not suited to be effective managers. By not understanding the difference we limit our potential.

Finding greater potential within yourself and the organization begins with understanding business systems and processes. Quality systems and processes establish structure and perception. They contribute to the basic human needs of trust and respect.

Effective leaders value and enforce systems and processes. They work diligently to eliminate random acts of poor judgement, silos, and unfortunate behaviors by the organization. Most importantly, systems and processes focus on the source of challenges rather than symptoms.

Culture

Cultural systems manage the boundaries and perception of both management and employees. The 360° Cultural System assesses the cultural health and values of a business.

High-capacity business cultures generally support three conditions.

1. Quality Team
2. Job Security
3. Competitive Compensation and Benefits

Here's what these three conditions mean to you.

1. Employees want and expect a quality team environment. Inconsistency, dysfunction, unequal performance accountability, and inadequate management practices do not support a quality team.

The fact is most quality employees leave a job because of inconsistencies and behaviors in their manager or organization rather than the job.

2. Employees want a permanent career and home. Job changes are disruptive and stressful for the employee. Management threats and inconsistent job security ultimately lead to attrition by even the best employees. Today, employees will not live in fear or in a world of retaliation in a tight job market.

Companies with continuous layoffs are victims. It's the absence of leadership.

3. Employees want to receive fair compensation and benefits. If the business culture is poor and filled with threats, no amount of compensation will retain a quality employee. Businesses with excessive employee attrition should first review their culture and business practices to determine the source of the attrition rather than increase their compensation.

Deliverables

Culture impacts the success of the company from the CEO downward to maintenance employees. Quality cultures simply achieve more objectives. They efficiently execute the strategy and tactics necessary to achieve the goal.

In fact, a quality culture contributes to employee and customer retention. And they allow potential leaders to become and remain leaders.

Customers expect quality, service, and value at a level of 100%, not 80%. Customer perception is influenced by employee perception.

Average is inconsistent in the business world. Customer loyalty depends on the company delivering predictable and sustainable deliverables.

It's always interesting to assess company culture and discover cultural health and customer retention share like metrics. When we benchmark cultural metrics, we can establish solutions and goals for improving our cultural health.

Quality cultures retain customers because of employee care and attention. The business avoids being on the hamster wheel of attrition. That's why effective leaders place so much value in their cultural dynamics.

Strategy

Strategy is a plan to achieve a goal. Strategy systems identify opportunities, challenges, and risk. Strategy building clarifies the goals and critical thinking of the management team and senior leadership.

Leaping on a goal and the supporting objectives without due diligence is characteristic of enterprises without genuine systems and processes.

The purpose of strategy is not only planning to accomplish a goal, but rather should the company even pursue the goal.

It's great to have a grand vision, and we need more grand visions. Unfortunately, executing a grand vision without strategic planning damages team, job security, and compensation. Employees see failure and dysfunction as a threat to job stability and compensation.

Summary

The overarching question for the reader is, why would a customer want to consistently purchase from your organization? I suggest it begins with quality leadership, culture, and strategy as the foundation for success.

Concepts to Ponder

1. Is the organization strategic in nature or tactical?
2. Does the business retain high performance employees?
3. Do customers view the company as a quality organization?

Article 6

Critical Thinking, Managing Through Chaos

These are challenging times for industry. Chaos and dysfunction surround us both externally and internally. Now's the time for leadership, culture management, and strategy.

For manufacturers, raw materials, packaging, energy, and equipment costs are still escalating. Internally, management and employees are faced with challenges in staffing, wages, and achieving performance expectations.

Until the catalysts of energy, inflation, and interest rates are resolved, it's going to be a bumpy ride. While distribution and customers don't like these conditions, they are forced to accept them, or go without. The alternative is to cease to exist.

Despite the turmoil, quality companies can grow.

The Chaos Syndrome

The Chaos Syndrome applies to management and employees as well. That is, chaos in decision making, expectations, performance, and behavior for both for management and employees. Ask any HR manager and they will tell you these are unusual times.

Chaos impacts organizational culture and perception in long term ways. Cultural chaos has substantial impact on employee health, stress, and family. And maybe your own passion for the business.

The pandemic exacted an enormous toll on business. Now, US policy is having the same effect. To survive we must improve, evolve, and adapt.

Critical Thinking

Critical thinking refers to the ability to analyze information objectively and make a reasoned judgment.

Management is compensated to achieve objectives. The more critical thinking that occurs the more likely we are to plan for challenges.

Quality organizations with strong models of leadership, culture, and strategy achieve more objectives. They have the ability and capacity to improve, evolve, and adapt. They are better prepared for events outside of their control.

Critical thinking depends on your model or perspective of the world. It influences how we analyze, evaluate, and prioritize opportunities and challenges.

Low performing organizations are challenged to improve, evolve, and adapt to chaos and dysfunction.

The fact is if your model of the world is okay with average or inconsistent performance, then that's what you receive.

Organizational boundaries influence perspective. If there are no boundaries in decision making, anything can happen. That's why well-defined vision, mission, and core value statements are a constant reminder to management of their boundaries.

Education is not a substitute for quality judgment. Those MBA's are helpful, but not a substitute for relationships, experience, and common sense. That's the conundrum business management faces.

I've noticed when management and employees are constantly reminded of company values, they tend to make more predictable and sustainable decisions.

Conversely, if value statements have little meaning to management, they have even less value to employees. The result is customers and suppliers establish negative perception of the business.

Management determines the effectiveness of the vision, mission, and core value statements. If management chooses to live by them, most often they enforce them. When value statements are out of sight and mind, so is critical thinking.

Five Contributors to Improve Critical Thinking

Effective Communication

Effective and consistent communication is the glue connecting management, employees, and customers. Diluted or flawed communication leads to the failure of employes to understand expectations.

Conversely, if management fails to listen to employees, communication fails. The final result is failure to achieve strategies and tactics.

Solution: Sharpen your message to be clear, concise, and relevant. Ask if team members understand the message and gain their feedback.

Revenue

Revenue is an outcome. Sure, we all have financial goals, it's the way of capitalism. Ultimately sales revenue is the result of multiple departments, teams, and individuals working together to satisfy customer expectations. It's not solely a sales function.

Customers expect 100% quality, service, and value on a consistent basis. A rating of poor in any of these three areas result in attrition. Customer attrition is a result of inconsistent performance.

And the fact is, repeat and loyal customers influence and deliver revenue achievement. When management is consistently achieving quality, service, and value, critical thinking advances as well.

Solution: Establish management systems and processes for every level of management.

Establish KPI's for Every Department

Key performance indicators (KPI's) measure and benchmark critical issues. KPI's apply metrics to every level of management and department.

We recommend 3-4 KPI's of the most critical objectives. Equal accountability applies to every level of the business. If a team is not performing, KPI's generally establish the why and why not.

Don't deceive yourself, other management members, employees, and customers all take notice of poor performance.

Solution: Establish KPI's at your top levels of management first. As they become effective, establish KPI's at all levels of the organization.

Company Culture

Company culture establishes perception with employees, customers, and suppliers. Culture management is a job function of every manager.

Healthy cultures are an indicator of customer perception. Satisfied customers collaborate well with customer service and sales.

Most importantly, healthy cultures better retain employees and customers. The Battle of Attrition is a constant contributor to financial stress.

Solution: Complete a 360° Organizational Assessment to understand the strengths and weaknesses of the organization.

Strategy

Effective strategies establish the course, speed, and achievement of the organization. There's nothing more demoralizing for employees when a strategy is doomed from the start.

Many times, strategy is understanding what a company has the capacity to accomplish and what it does not. Throwing darts is a costly cultural and financial move.

Solution: Planning requires time, accurate information, and accountability. Ensure your team is asking the right questions about the goal.

Concepts to Ponder

1. In general, is management communication effective in the organization?
2. Does the Chaos Syndrome reign in your organization?
3. Do customer receive 100% quality, service, and value on a consistent basis.

Article 7

Fewer Teachable Moments

Teachable moments in business generally occur after a failed strategy or colossal disaster comes to light. It's the brief window in time where management reflects on the absence of effective leadership, culture, or strategy.

Defer, deny, defend. Finger pointing, blame games, and excuses seek to coverup the mess.

Management is instantly on high alert, figuring out how to bury the news. And news travels twice as fast when employees are accused as being a contributor to the teachable moment.

Customers shake their heads and wonder what management is thinking. Employees question the capacity of management. And the bitter word of attrition becomes part of the company vocabulary.

Certainly, every business has some degree of risk. Every business has differing levels of tolerance for risk. And some businesses manage risk well. They understand managements responsibility is to consistently assess the risks, rewards, and value before they leap.

Leadership

Senior management's role is to establish goals, approve effective strategies, and achieve positive outcomes. This means senior management consistently facilitates accountability, assesses risk, and remains within the boundaries of the vision, mission, and core values.

Intriguingly, teachable moments most often occur when company goals, strategies, and tactics exceed the capacity of the management team. Exceeding the capacity of the management team means critical thinking, systems and processes, and effective communication are most likely absent.

Quality leaders separate themselves from task management. They focus on cultivating and assessing customer relationships. They identify opportunity and innovation. They are both stewards and guardians of company culture. And they assess goals and strategies for accurate value.

Culture

Employee perception is the face of company culture. Perception is cultural reality. Perception is what employees interpret and feel about the organization. Quality cultures result in more goals and strategies being achieved. And quality cultures are better focused on retention rather than attrition.

Employee ambassadors communicate company perception to customers with every transaction. Company culture, both good and bad, establishes predictable value at every level.

And considering this, quality customers want to engage with like suppliers. Less grief, and it's simply more profitable.

Culture management begins with assessing employee perception. 360° Organizational Assessments establish and validate fact or fiction with evidence. Factual evidence in ten assessment areas benchmark the cultural health of the organization.

Culture management delivers consistent and actionable evidence. It distinguishes the why and how of improving perception within, and external to the organization. And from my experience, the leading culprits generally include lack of systems and processes, accountability, and communication.

Strategy

Strategy: A method, a plan, or a decision-making model to <u>consistently</u> achieve desired goals.

The vast majority of small and medium business organizations conduct strategic planning on the fly. Some work out, others not so well. Poor decisions have a cost.

The challenge with strategic planning on the fly is processes seldom cascade down to subordinate managers and key employees. These managers don't learn how to make a quality decision.

Eventually, subordinate managers move to organizations who better value their trust and decision-making skills. The intellectual capacity of the organization is limited to a few at the top. The company is trapped in the employee attrition mode.

46

Most of the companies I consult with have a strategic planning process or model they follow. No one model is exactly right or wrong, but they work for that organization. But the result is, teachable moments are minimized.

Generally, effective strategic planning shares three conditions to prevent teachable moments.

1. Is the goal relevant and concise, and reflect the company core competencies?
2. Does the strategy meet the conditions of the company vision, mission, and core values?
3. Does the strategy achieve the goal and bring significant value to the organization and customers without undue risk?

The word No, is the most powerful word in the human dictionary. No, minimizes flawed strategies which contributes to toxic cultures. No, supports accountability and planning. No, better manages risk. No, makes all of us better leaders.

Teachable Moments

Teachable moments come at price. Profit, culture, and competitive advantage to name a few. Most importantly, management frustration, stress, and behaviors are magnified by teachable moments. And to think, most teachable moments are preventable.

Concepts to Ponder

1. Does your organization experience frequent teachable moments?

2. Does your organization effectively manage risk?
3. Does your organization practice strategic planning on the fly?

Article 8

Pulling Back the Curtain for Growth

Every company has challenges. Some choose to deny challenges. Some defer challenges, hoping they will improve. Others confront challenges and solve them.

Rarely are major challenges a secret. Employees and customers are generally aware of challenges. And often, so are competitors.

Employee Perception

Employee perception is established when management denies or defers challenges. Employee perception attacks both culture and strategy. It undermines leadership.

Customers establish perception about quality, service, and value. They establish perception about supplier competency, capacity, and value. The customer chooses whether they want to invest more or less with a supplier.

Many times, customer perception is why all-important innovation fails. Customers predetermine their purchase risk before innovation is even presented. Unless the innovation is substantial and the rewards are high, challenged suppliers don't get a chance to bat.

Pulling Back the Curtain

Do you remember, "The great and powerful Oz in the 1939 movie, Wizard of Oz?" The great Oz was an all-powerful magician, no mortal had ever seen.

"Toto" the dog pulled back the curtain for Dorthy and her friends exposing the truth. Alas, the great Oz was a mere mortal. And Toto removed the blinders of illusion the Great Oz hid behind. Eventually, Oz made good by giving away a heart, intelligence, and courage.

What's Behind Your Curtain?

Again, every company has challenges. If your goal is growth, what are your liabilities and illusions?

The 360° Organizational Assessment is one important tool to Pull Back the Curtain. It exposes the limits of capacity and structure from the employee point of view. The 360° Organizational Assessment process distinguishes between source and symptom, fact versus fiction.

The assessment identifies and benchmarks ten (10) areas in management, culture, and strategy. These ten areas essentially measure the structural capacity of the organization.

We ask actionable and relevant questions in our 360° Organizational Assessment. Then we apply systems and processes to correct the deficiencies. And to be clear, it's not about throwing management under the bus. It's about continuous improvement.

The 360° Organizational Assessment process benchmarks improvement and distinguishes between source and symptom. It's a tool to measure capacity. From this information, Tacticware builds a solid structure of systems in management, culture, and strategy.

Concepts to Ponder

1. What is customer perception about quality, service, and value regarding your business?
2. What are your truthful liabilities and illusions about the organization?
3. Does your business confront challenges or deny they exist?

Article 9

Reimagine Your Organizational Quality

Every business has challenges. Most challenges have solutions, and some do not. As managers and leaders, it's important to reflect on the good, bad, and ugly components of your business.

These are challenging times for many companies. When you're in the middle of battle day after day, we become hardened to dysfunction and chaos.

Eventually we become accepting of chaos. We also become accepting of stress and emotional baggage tagging along with chaos.

Devil is in the Details

Consider this, sales revenue is a result. Customer loyalty is a result. Profit margins are a result. Each depends on effective management leadership, culture, and strategy to achieve success.

The wildcard in all of this is the quality of the organization. Quality organizations understand the "devil is in the details." Most often it's the lack of management attention or understanding to the details creating chaos and dysfunction.

What's so interesting for many companies is assessing customer and employee retention. So often, high quality customers and employees don't leave because of price or compensation. They leave because of organizational quality.

Tweaking Your Management Approach

Effective management systems work to accomplish the details. Communication, best practices, and expectations follow a prescribed course. We have learned big course corrections are generally not helpful.

Small and steady course corrections allow the business, management, and employees to adjust to the system's approach. Chaos and dysfunctional behaviors lessen. Customer transactions and relationships improve.

Systems tend to take the emotion out of business and relationships. Systems deal with facts.

Facilitators

Business systems allow management to become facilitators of leadership, culture and strategy. That is, managers are able to focus on opportunity, rather than achieve tasks.

Employees are able to achieve their job function. Strategies and objectives are better executed.

Stress and burnout are no longer a daily event. Organizational quality becomes the objective of facilitators.

System Results

What we observe is sales revenue, customer loyalty, and profitability improve. As organizational quality improves, so does performance. Both satisfy customers and employees.

Success comes one step at a time. Management discussion, collaboration, and accountability make systems successful. Everyone works within the system.

Management teams learning together exposes the good, bad, and ugly. Management teams' problem solving together creates solutions and sustainability. Chaos and dysfunction become infrequent events.

Concepts to Ponder

1. Does your business manage details effectively?
2. Does your organization utilize systems to manage employee and business practices?
3. Is your company managed on facts or emotion?

Section 2

Overview of Customers, Revenue, and Relationships

Customers, revenue, and relationships all share a common denominator, trust. Without trust customers fail to order and reorder. Customers mitigate their risk.

The primary source of trust for customers is consistent quality, service, and value. Inconsistent quality, service, and value creates distrust.

Employees are the communicators of trust. With every transaction, employees communicating the core values of the organization. Honorable and consistently applied core values speaks for the organization.

Experience

Recently we replaced two air conditioners that were simply worn out. Several HVAC contractors bid the replacement cost of the units. Some were high and others were low.

The HVAC contractor we ultimately chose was higher in price than other bidders. The representative that came out to the house was thorough, specific, and clear about the process. He was passionate about the quality, service, and value his company provided.

His professionalism was outstanding. His communication skills were over the top. His marketing brochure was professional and detailed.

I then asked him about the organization and staff. They had a large number of technicians and support staff. Their service vans were clean and polished as were their uniforms.

I asked about what I could expect during the installation and cleanup. He explained every detail.

Ownership

Then I asked the representative how long he had been with the company. He stated 14 years, from the very beginning. I asked if he had an equity position in the company and he responded, yes.

The representative turned out to be the owner with 100% equity. This was the owner of a successful business who communicated his vision, mission, and core values to a potential customer.

Then the HVAC installation crew arrived. The crew chief and employees were respectful with me and each other. Every employee reflected the owners core values.

Every detail was completed on time in perfect working order. My customer satisfaction and loyalty is 100%.

The point of this commentary is, Confident and Bold Leadership is a choice.

Concepts to Ponder

1. Does your management and employees take ownership of, and communicate company values?

2. What message is your customer facing employees conveying to customers?
3. Would your top 10 volume customer provide a satisfactory or superior rating?

Article 10

Customer Relevance: How Relevant is Your Business to Customers?

Introduction

How relevant is your business to customers? Do customers see your organization as a leader in innovation, quality, and service?

Is your company team,

1. Really a team, or an organized gang?
2. Consistently staffed with professionals delivering solutions.
3. Does customer satisfaction and loyalty metrics align with top ranking competitors?

Ask your customers what drivers influence their purchasing decisions. Too many times, companies become irrelevant to customers because of inconsistent leadership, culture, and innovation.

It's not price that kills the notion of relevancy, it's the quality of the organization.

Quality organizations have three things in common, effective leadership, culture, and communication.

Unfortunately, one doesn't code their way to leadership, nor interpersonal relationships. Technology is simply a mechanism for efficiency, data management, and robotic tasks. It's not a substitute for leadership, TEAM, or collaborative communication.

Leadership

Recently I was with a manufacturing client discussing his suppliers. One supplier to the organization was under review.

According to the client purchasing agent, the supplier had incorrectly assumed the relationship was in good standing, and also assumed service levels met expectations.

We also learned this supplier had not introduced innovation for some period of time. Another concern was poor communication from various departments within the supplier.

Interestingly, the products this supplier offered were priced competitively, but the aggregate value of the supplier had diminished. The supplier had slowly become irrelevant.

We suggest the aggregate value of the organization is determined by its leadership. Every department and employee in the company is responsible for customer satisfaction and relevancy.

Pivot to Greater Relevancy

If a company plans to pivot and grow its customer relevancy, leadership should understand the truth about the organization. Effective discovery processes use 360° organizational assessments and customer surveys. They discover real facts and evidence regarding leadership, company culture, and customer expectations.

Relevant companies develop actionable strategies for improvement. Companies destined for irrelevancy do nothing. They file assessment intelligence away as toxic, never to be seen again.

Effectively pivoting from irrelevancy requires an actionable strategy.

Actionable strategy is one that is well crafted and executable. It influences and Upskills both leadership and employees.

Culture

Your culture is your brand." Culture influences the aggregate value of the brand. Positive cultures embrace communication, collaboration, and interpersonal relationships. Positive cultures are also focused on continuous improvement in job skills and career development.

Relevant companies are finely tuned to their cultural metrics. Cultural improvement delivers greater productivity, employee retention, and customer satisfaction.

Culture is also an indicator of company business practices. Employees are a transmitter of culture and a direct line to establishing customer perception.

Diversity and inter-company career development work to grow relevancy. Quality cultures take better care of customer relationships. Critical thinking is simply dispensed by more people.

Organizational Quality

Quality is a measurement, or perception of company products and services. Organizational quality is measurement of long-term values, achievement, sustainability, and employee investment.

Relevant companies are focused on the careful balance of quality. Irrelevant companies struggle to differentiate between the two kinds of quality.

> *We choose our customers. We choose our risk. We choose our profit margin. Everything is a choice.*

Effective organizations generally take the notion of quality to radically different destinations. The real difference is TEAM. Quality employees better deliver quality goods and services for a greater value.

Customers view their relationship and investment as productive and relevant. When suppliers are solely focused on product or service quality, they fail to meet customer expectations.

Innovation

Relevancy is determined by the value suppliers bring in the form of innovation. Effective innovation delivers new value to the customer. It's also an opportunity to expand the professional relationship.

Leadership and culture combined drive the company's ability to deliver innovation. Leaders who are out of touch with customers fail to recognize the value and importance of effective innovation.

Passive cultures are hard pressed to value innovation. They see innovative products and services as another task rather than the future.

Passive cultures are generally resistant to change. They are a major contributor to company irrelevancy. The fallacy is wages is the source of cultural passivity. The real source is leadership and expectations.

Relevancy

When companies cease to be relevant, customers look elsewhere. It's simple, they are mitigating risk.

Effective leadership, culture, and communication are the fundamental source of quality. Leaders decide whether to be relevant or irrelevant.

Ultimately, the competitive nature of capitalism eventually determines company status. Relevancy or perish.

Concepts to Ponder

1. How would you rate the overall quality of products and or services of the company?
2. How would you rate the total quality of the organization?
3. How would customers rate the total quality of the organization?

Article 11

Customer Loyalty

Management is challenged every year with delivering sales and earnings growth. The rules have now evolved because customers want more than just a competitive price - they have a whole litany of expectations.

Companies that expect to gain or retain competitive advantage must adjust their business models and message to compensate. Over the last decade, companies have invested in technology to gain efficiencies. ERP and CRM software developed information-based companies.

But now the question is:

How do companies better use market intelligence to grow customer trust and loyalty?

Customers tell us the answer is quality people. We know it's selecting, training, and retaining the right people.

But, in reality, growing customer loyalty is much more complicated than this piece of the puzzle. In this Article, I discuss a strategy for uniting key needs in the relationship building process - Enterprise Capacity Language.

Customer Types

Companies have three kinds of customers

- Customer Advocates
- Customer Neutrals
- Customer Critics

Customer Types

<u>Customer Advocates</u> offer predictable purchase histories and loyalty to the company.

<u>Customer Neutrals</u> purchase on a frequent basis but have no real loyalty.

<u>Customer critics</u> are those who purchase because they must.

Customer Advocates

Customer advocates are loyal customers for a number of reasons. They can be large or small in size. They are satisfied with the quality, service and value of the product or service.

Additionally, they welcome innovation and collaboration. Customer advocates are the reference every company wished to document and pass on to new potential customers.

Customer Neutrals

Customer neutrals are customer without significant loyalty. They generally have other suppliers with the same products or services.

Customer neutrals are vulnerable to competitive threat and are frequently solicited by the competition. Scary is when you learn your high-volume customers are really neutrals without any true loyalty to the company. Really scary is when you learn price is not the reason.

Customer Critics

Customer critics are customers who purchase because they must. If they could replace a supplier with another favorite, they would do so.

Risk management is of great concern to most companies. Risk management is sometimes limited to procurement, supply chain, and security rather than company behavior. In this case, the risk of losing a large customer is significant challenge.

So, what do loyal customers really care about?

- Quality and consistent products and services
- Innovation
- Communication / Collaboration / Professionalism
- Service
- Value / price

The Catalyst for Change — Growing Customer Advocates

Customers expect 100% achievement to earn a trusting and loyal relationship. Customer loyalty and trust is everything because it's bankable.

Quality customers simply don't want dysfunction and poor business practices as part of their income stream for good reason, this behavior is unpredictable and costly.
Customers want to do business with suppliers that generate

profitable outcomes and collaborative relationships. This concept extends to sales agencies as an extension of the company sales force.

We often hear from new clients about business losses due to price. Many times, after investigation we find price wasn't the culprit, it was company business practices.

Customer attrition is not only devastating to the financial balance sheet, but to employee morale. Eventually employee perception becomes tarnished, which influences company culture.

Enterprise Capacity Language

Enterprise Capacity Language (ECL) is an approach that can help your team better transition your customers toward Client Advocate status.

At the crux of it, ECL is about management and employees using information to grow relationships. With ECL, management and employees center on the source of challenges rather than the symptoms and are empowered to perform well.

Here is the challenge and a key component of ECL— every company employee that touches the customer influences perception. It's not solely a function of the sales relationship.

Tip: Perception is customer reality. Every contact your customer has with a member of your company must be positive - which includes R/D, production, supply chain, administration, and most importantly, management. No exceptions.

Where Technology Fits In

Industry is in a race to implement new technology. The real race is about selecting and retaining quality management and employees to use technology effectively.

Our observation: companies often find it easier to implement technology and cost cutting efficiencies rather than improve the quality of employees and the organization.

> *The notion technology alone is going to solve a company's ills is nonsense. Rather, it's quality people using technology effectively that achieves objectives."*

Sure, companies need to be highly efficient and price competitive, but there should be a balanced approach between people and technology.

Enterprise Resource Planning (ERP) and Customer Resource Management (CRM) software create vast amounts of information. They operate most effectively when quality people collect, interpret, communicate and apply the intelligence to existing market conditions. Clearly, managing risk is important and companies need critical thinking to gain a competitive edge.

Tip: ERP and CRM software harness a plethora of data that you can utilize in real-time. Empower your Quality Employees to act on that data as they best see fit, whether that means rewarding return customers or even company employees. Don't stymie via red tape and bureaucracy.

Company Culture

Company culture is determined by employees and management. Employees quickly determine if company culture is compatible or flawed. Failing to meet the language of the core values/ vision/ mission statements plants the seeds of discontent. The absence of effective planning, communication, and execution translate to both customers and employees.

Some of the most compelling evidence is when the company loses a key employee over business practices, rather than salary. The fact is both customers and employees recognize the significance of quality. Why purchase from, or work for a company with challenges?

Legacy behaviors and business practices influence customer perception. Just because we have always done it this way, doesn't make it right.

Quality employees want to see the company thrive and prosper. Connecting all levels of the company to a single performance language includes management, production leaders, supply chain, marketing, and sales. One number that says we are on course with customer expectations, or we have work to do.

Tip: Survey feedback both from customers and your own employees. Anonymously or publicly, internally or by bringing in an outside, unbiased source like Tacticware. Give members a voice for innovation, and you can proactively resolve any potential issues.

Final Thoughts

An ECL or "Enterprise Capacity Language" approach bridges the gap between employees, technology, and customer loyalty - it's a common language of performance focused on creating Customer Advocates.

ECL encourages employee self-management, accountability, and achievement while addressing the needs of the customer and company. We believe that ECL is the catalyst for sales revenue and earnings growth.

Concepts to Ponder

1. What is your organizations customer performance language?
2. Do any or many of the company's largest customers share a neutral position on quality?
3. Has the organization ever lost a great customer over poor business practices?

Article 12

Sales Revenue Growth, Becoming Customer Centric

Sales revenue growth is generally top of mind for most management teams. First, it increases shareholder value and financials. Secondly, sales revenue growth allows for reinvestment in people, innovation, and facilities.

It's not accidental or magic. Sustainable and predictable sales revenue growth is a result of quality leadership, culture, and strategy. When they effectively work together, the organization develops competitive advantage.

When sales revenue is strong every department looks like a positive contributor. When sales are challenged, departmental imperfections are illuminated. The financial reality is that when sales revenue is off plan, it's sometimes a result of other internal performance challenges.

Sales revenue growth and profitability are a result.

In our view, each and every department contributes to sales revenue growth, not merely the sales team. Each department contributes to competitive advantage and customer loyalty.

All Eyes on the Customer

Organizational quality is not just about product quality, it's the result of every department focused on improving the customer experience. Customer satisfaction is transactional.

Customer loyalty is earned from the total experience and perception of the organization.

When customers have positive transactions and perception time after time, customer loyalty grows. When transactions are inconsistent for any reason, so goes customer satisfaction and ultimately, some level of customer loyalty.

Customer Retention

What is <u>not</u> true is sales departments have 100% responsibility for customer retention. This occurs when company business practices are responsible for customer attrition.

More often, it's because the organization failed to be customer centric. That is, when the entire organization fails to be focused on customer satisfaction.

Quality customers limit their exposure to risk. Sometimes customers use price as an excuse. More often, it's about deficient business practices and communication from departments other than sales.

When customer attrition exceeds new customer acquisition, sales revenue diminishes. It's the leaky bucket syndrome.

The following are five top influencers of sales revenue growth.

Communication

Customers want to trust suppliers. Suppliers effectively communicating with customers build positive perception. Often, positive perception allows suppliers to become preferred suppliers. These suppliers gain competitive advantage.

The same holds true for employees. Quality employees want to trust company management. They want to communicate with customers and know management is supportive and working to solve their challenges.

Enterprises with superior internal communication skills build positive employee perception. Employee retention is a key performance indicator of communication quality. And remember, every employee is a customer ambassador.

Failure to communicate really means an absence of quality.

Communication is a cornerstone of leadership, cultural environment, and effective strategies.

Does your organization effectively communicate with both customers and employees?

Sales Team Quality - Focus on Strategic Accounts

Strategic accounts generally have three criteria.

1. Those with the greatest potential for significant and profitable sales revenue volume
2. Those with the ability to become satisfied and loyal customers
3. Those who invite innovation

If the customer profit margins are so low there's no room for sustainable profit, is the strategic customer really strategic?

Organizations choose their customers to solicit. Quality customers realize low price suppliers have liabilities. They often mean poor quality, service, and support. Fair profit means fair value for both parties.

Sure, smaller accounts are generally easier to sell. Every company needs an abundance of smaller quality customers who are loyal, pay their bills on time, and are open to innovation.

However, smaller customers often do not have the capacity to significantly grow a company's overall business. Generally, it takes a substantial number of smaller accounts to equal a strategic account. And overall, the cost of sale is generally higher with smaller accounts.

Does your sales team have the capacity and skills to sell strategic customers?

Distribution Quality- Order/Fill/Ship

Customers expect 100% of their orders to be consistently and accurately filled and shipped on time. Industry purchasing agents generally report a significant amount of their time is spent tracking down incomplete or late orders.

Suppliers consistently achieving close to 100% customer order-fill-ship gain positive customer perception. Quality suppliers form a preferred relationship with customers. To be fair, it's not a perfect world.

73

Occasional challenges are different than frequent challenges.

Inconsistency forces customer purchasing departments to become indifferent to suppliers. Suppliers become irrelevant with inconsistent business practices.

Then there's larger customers who measure order, fill, and ship KPI's (key performance indicators). These customers do understand source versus symptom.

If we place ourselves in the customers chair, why would we risk inconsistent performance from a supplier?

Does your organization order-fill-ship performance indicators approach 100%?

Customer Service Quality

Customer Service is a communication gateway. I've found the department is a barometer for customer perception and satisfaction.

What happens when identical customer challenges happen daily or frequently? Is customer service solving for source or symptom?

Today companies use technology for order transactions. However, it's Customer Service who interprets customer challenges, and resolves complaints. They contribute to establishing customer perception of the organization.

When companies fail to distinguish between source or symptom, customers go elsewhere.

Does your organization measure and benchmark the customer experience?

Product or Service Quality

Customers assess the quality of their product or service with every order. Realistically, it's challenging to be at 100% in manufacturing or service.

However, effective Quality Assurance should identify challenges before they reach the customer.

Quality Assurance is the gatekeeper of the manufacturing/customer relationship.

How customers value the brand certainly is influenced by quality. Inconsistent quality contributes to customer attrition and negative sales revenue growth.

Again, it's not a perfect world, but we can mitigate customer risk though best practices.

Does your organization measure and benchmark product or service quality?

Summary

Sales revenue growth and profitability are a result. When all departments focus on achieving customer satisfaction, sales revenue expands.

Positive customer perception allows for greater innovation opportunities. By providing more goods or services, the supplier becomes a more valuable resource.

Concepts to Ponder

1. Does the company manage and monitor customer perception?
2. Does the company sales team distinguish between strategic customers and good customers?
3. Is quality assurance a priority or afterthought in the company?

Article 13

Financial Capacity: The Impact of Company Culture on the Financial Statement.

In this Article, we discuss "Financial Capacity: The Impact of Company Culture on the Financial Statement." The article includes why and how culture management sets the boundaries and limitations of company financials. We will focus on the following topics:

1. Innovation - R&D Expense
2. Customer Satisfaction And Retention - Revenue
3. Management Effectiveness - Revenue - Strategy And Performance
4. Employee Productivity And Retention - Wages And Benefits
5. Working Environment - Wages And Benefits
6. Risk Management - Insurance Expense

Whether your business is B2B or B2C, effective cultural management shapes profitability and shareholder value.

Five-Star Performance: Greater Expectations

Today, companies must set greater expectations if they expect to succeed. I suggest businesses consider the Five Star Standard. It is a simple rating system that applies to both customers and employees.

I encourage clients to move their thinking beyond "average." Average in traditional rating scales is a C. With the Five Star Rating System, think of each Star with a value of 20%.

If we are to gain competitive advantage, the least acceptable rating is a four-star rating. After all, if we do not stretch to improve, we erode.

The Star Rating System is a model of simplicity. It benchmarks both customer and employee perception of the company.

5 Stars- Superior
4 Stars- Satisfactory
3 Stars- Inconsistent
2 Stars- Needs improvement
1 Star - Critical

To sum up the Star Ratings:

- **Five Star performance** means consistently superior customer and employee satisfaction and retention. Five Star relationships generally result in a greater pool of strategic customer relationships. Five Star performance generally results in greater employee retention and productivity. Strong cultures are generally proactive to risk management.

  The result is superior financial capacity.

- **Four Star performance** means satisfactory. There may be some restrained and/or inconsistent satisfaction or trust from customers and employees. The result is moderate financial capacity.

- **Three Stars or less performance** generally means inconsistent, unpredictable, and sometimes incompatible customer and employee satisfaction. Competitors are probably winning both customers and employees. The result is limited financial capacity.

Rating Organizational Culture

"Organizational Culture is a system of shared values, beliefs, and business practices." - Investopedia

As we have discussed in previous Articles, a Cultural Management System governs how people and teams behave, communicate, plan, engage, and perform within the organization.

It measures and benchmarks organizational perception from all employees through a Star Rating process. Company vision, mission, and core values all work together to establish cultural expectations.

A Cultural Management System also governs how management and employees communicate quality, innovation, value, service, and relationships to external customers. It measures and benchmarks customer satisfaction through a Star Rating process.

Every employee is a cultural ambassador. With every customer transaction, the Star Rating is in play. If the company expects to maximize its financial capacity, a Five Star Rating is necessary.

Actionable Suggestions

Please consider the following:

1. What is the customer attrition rate?
2. What is the employee attrition rate?
3. What significant financial resources have been expended to restore customer confidence due to quality, supply chain, distribution, or relationship challenges?
4. What financial resources have been expended to correct strategy, management, or human resource challenges?

Pivot Your Thinking

Continuous improvement is necessary to achieve our financial goals. Culture management moves culture from a subjective ideal, to a managed discipline. Look at your toughest competitor and determine how these topics influence your financial status.

#1: Innovation

Company culture plays an important role in innovation. Successful companies invest significant resources into R&D. Some investments are an extension of existing products. For others, it may leap beyond its core competencies.

Innovation accomplishes three objectives. First, it provides new income streams. Second, it creates the opportunity to collaborate and innovate with existing customers. Third, innovation provides the opportunity to discover new customers.

Five Star customer relationships encourage and support greater investment in innovation. They are the first customers to approach with innovation.

Sometimes strategic customers don't share the same love. We have found, with some clients, their best and most strategic customers rated the company as a 2-3 Star Rated supplier. Company leaders are sometimes surprised with this dose of reality.

The truth is innovation often struggles with existing customers. Customers with 1-2-3 Star ratings sometimes choose not to purchase innovation from the company. Why invest with suppliers that are providing limited value?

New customers are generally willing to risk very little from unknown suppliers. New customers don't know you. Nor do they trust you.

How frequently do new customers purchase from your company? Statistically, sales closure rates on new customers purchasing innovation are very low for most industries.

Companies with 4-5 Star cultures generally have a firm handle on strategic customer relationships. They are generally the most successful innovators. They achieve the greatest return on the R&D investment.

Remember, every employee is a company ambassador. Company ambassadors are viral communicators of culture.

Actionable Suggestions

Please consider the following:

1. How successful has the distribution of company innovation been with regard to strategic customers?
2. What has been the Return on Investment regarding innovation?
3. How many company customers are both Five Star rated and strategic?

#2: Customer Satisfaction and Retention

Revenue and earnings erode quickly with the loss of a strategic customer. Customers often leave because of company business practices, not price. Price is just an easy excuse.

Business practices are a function of culture. More often than not, price is a muted response to a bad experience from an employee or business practice. Customers reach their limit of bad experiences, opening the door for competitors to "win over" the customer.

Profitability and earnings erode slowly with the loss of a smaller customers. The company is forced to not only replace customer attrition, but to increase growth as well.

Growth and revenue profits are impacted by culture. Hypothetically, if the company:

- Experiences 10% customer attrition
- And expect +8% sales plan growth
- It requires +18% in real growth to meet plan

Generally, +18% growth is a real challenge for most companies. The fact is with excessive customer attrition, most companies never achieve plan goals through organic growth.

Hence, acquisition becomes the growth model. Financial risk increases through greater leverage of company indebtedness.

The takeaway here is when companies improve company culture, customer satisfaction and retention improve. Company revenue increases as does new opportunities.

Actionable Suggestions

Please consider the following:

1. What is the Star Rating of your top strategic customers?
2. If the Star Rating is low, what is the real truth? Call the customer personally and determine the facts.

#3: Management Effectiveness

Leadership and management are two distinctly different skill sets.

- Leadership is consistently engaged with its customers, management, employees, and operational environment to increase company value.
- Management is consistently engaged in processes and systems to increase company value.

The Five Star Rating System performs as a benchmark of culture management. The Five Star System identifies and measures five areas of customer satisfaction. It also identifies ten (10) areas of employee perception and satisfaction. This allows for a way to use facts and evidence as a way to effectively understand and manage culture.

The real sign of a Five Star culture is when leaders and managers cease being "firefighters" and actually have the time to lead and manage. The "fires" of dysfunction, lackluster performance, and poor communication dim.

When leadership and management are better able to focus on strategic decisions, financial capacity improves. Priorities align with meaningful results.

Company leadership is better able to collaborate with strategic customers and facilitate the growth of its team. Perception and culture improvements diminish risk.

Actionable Suggestions

Please consider the following:

1. When did leadership last spend significant time with strategic customers?
2. Does company leadership maintain consistent customer relationships?

#4: Employee Productivity & Retention

Employee attrition has tremendous financial liability. Employee wages and benefits, training, and customer relationships all have a price. Employee attrition also influences management, productivity, risk, and company culture.

Superior cultures have a defined employee selection process. This process identifies the right person for the right job.

We hear from some managers they don't have sufficient time to manage a selection process, as they enjoy another day of "fighting fires." But the real fact is that selecting quality employees is key to culture management.

Recruiting and selecting productive employees begins with an accurate job description. Identifying primary objectives and activities allow the company to target specific skill sets.

Highly effective Candidate Assessments allow management to compare specific candidate skills, knowledge, and behaviors to a comprehensive job description. This style of assessment is very helpful in selecting the right candidates for the right job.

Other less effective Candidate Assessments identify basic personality traits and compare them to a broad job description. We ask you to consider the real expense of a toxic hire when considering using Candidate Assessments.

Companies promoting from within their own ranks should understand a great individual performer may not make a great manager. Skill sets do not always transfer, nor the ability to facilitate the success of subordinates.

On-boarding is not training.

Effective on-boarding contributes to employee retention. Leadership is responsible for effective on-boarding to explain the company's vision, mission, and core values.

The reason is accountability. Leadership is responsible for communicating company values and expectations so that every employee ambassador has the correct facts regarding company culture. Often times core values and expectations are lost in translation.

Effective job training provides knowledge, skills, and expectations. We recommend every training session also provide cultural reinforcement. The facts are employees value and expect effective training. They fear failure and stagnation.

Companies providing expert job training, apprentice programs, certification programs, and educational resources retain more employees. They attract new employees with greater skill sets and talent.

#5: Working Environment

Cultural Environment: Incubator of Employee Productivity

Five Star cultures deliver greater employee productivity. Part of the reason is superior communication, training, and accountability.

Fair accountability means all employees are held to equal expectations. There is mutual respect and trust among team members and management.

Believe it or not, fair and equal accountability are among the greatest complaints we have discovered in employee assessments in companies of all sizes. Fair and equal accountability supports the notion of team, rather than employee gangs.

People are fragile. Despite all the rhetoric about people and job expectations, not much has really changed over time. Quality people expect team, job security, and fair compensation and benefits. Exactly in that order.

Most companies are a mixture of generations. Some generations communicate differently. Some have a differing sense of time management. Five Star cultures treat everyone with realistic expectations and equal accountability.

Poor employee perception is an incubator of toxic employees. They either leave or infect the organization. If companies are to retain quality employees, the cultural environment must be positive.

#6: Company Risk Management

Risk is everywhere. Risk concerns exist throughout every organization. Financially, safety violations, data hacking, excessive insurance premiums, supply chain losses, and loss of revenue are sometimes indicators of a Star Rating of 1-2-3.

4-5 Star Rated companies better manage departmental risk. It's a priority for management and employees who are more accountable. Most importantly, management and employees are more proactive to overcome challenges and adversity.

Workers' Safety

In our experience within various industries, we have observed that companies with a 4-5 Star Rating consistently operate with fewer employee accidents. In those organizations, Safety First training and accountability has been a first priority of leadership, management, and employees.

Effective communication, respect, and accountability are key components of a strong culture. Strong cultures have engaged employees who seek to be the best and perform the safest course of action.

Intellectual Property Risk

All companies are vulnerable to computer hacking or compromised systems. Our observation is 4-5 Star Rated Companies are more proactive and diligent in assessing technology and intellectual property risks.

Leadership and management have more time to develop effective policies and procedures. They are also able to create an evolving process which learns from the last experience. Lower Star Rated companies repeat the same lesson time and again.

4-5 Star Rated companies generally tend to have fewer technology challenges. For many, there is a plan and process for education, updates, and best practices.

Financial Predictability - Managed Growth

Financial predictability influences banking and financial relationships. From a lender's perspective, cash intensive companies and inventory credit lines are influenced by predictable revenue. The source of predictable revenue is culture management.

For investors, well-managed growth generally indicates predictable results. Wide swings in revenue, liabilities, and earnings are sometimes an indicator of challenges. Why invest in a leadership and management team that is off course?

4-5 Star Rated companies generally have developed a larger pool of strategic customers. They are better able to predict and manage their financial status. EBITDA (earnings before interest, taxes, depreciation, and amortization) values are generally more significant and stable.

3 Star Rated companies are sometimes more inconsistent. Customers and employees recognize the inconsistency. Inconsistency is expensive and dysfunctional to customers.

Quality employees view inconsistency as a lack of leadership. When a better opportunity arrives, quality customers and employees move up and out. So does revenue and productivity.

1-2 Star Rated companies sometimes reside in chaos and mayhem. The business environment is uncomfortable and unpredictable. Oftentimes leadership and management are caught in an endless loop. Financial predictability varies from day to day.

Actionable Suggestions

Please consider the following:

1. Where does your company exist financially in the Five Star Rating System?
2. What are your financial limitations from a lender's perspective?

Conclusion

Throughout this Article I have discussed the relationship of culture management and financial capacity.

Our article included the Five Star Rating System. This system measures and benchmarks customer and employee perception and satisfaction.

Star Rating System

5 Stars- Superior
4 Stars- Satisfactory
3 Stars- Inconsistent
2 Stars- Needs improvement
1 Star - Critical

We encouraged clients to move their thinking beyond "average." Average in traditional rating scales is a C. With the Five Star Rating System, think of each Star with a value of 20%. If we are to gain competitive advantage, the least acceptable rating is a four-star rating.

We identified these contributors to financial capacity. We also provided tips and questions to identify challenges and opportunities in culture management.

Concepts to Ponder

1. What is the financial liability to the company from employees operating at the inconsistent or average level?

2. Does senior management hold all employees equally accountable with regard to job performance and core values?
3. Does the organization introduce innovation with a blanket approach or a strategic customer approach?

Article 14

Customer Relationships- Do We Know or Assume Our Customer Relationships?

Quality customer relationships drive sales revenue, earnings, and vision. Often times company management assumes positive customer relationships exist. They take the approach that no complaints equate to satisfied customers.

Many companies rely primarily on sales departments to maintain customer relationships. Sales department reporting and steady orders are the primary source of information regarding customer satisfaction. When a salesperson reports a customer relationship is fine, and the customer continues to order, then management moves on to fight larger fires.

Assumption is an action word for some management teams. Assumption is an indicator of the level of company leadership. Leadership teams focused on facts rather than assumptions generally walk a different path. Leadership relying on assumption generally exists in a world of financial dysfunction.

Service and retail industries survey (B2C) customers to determine customer satisfaction with every transaction. The consistent question is, "Did we perform well or not?" Without sounding negative, how many of these companies actually improve their customer practices from survey data?

As a customer, what is it like to contact the company or complete a survey and never see any improvement?

Leadership

Business to Business (B2B) companies should maintain a top-to-top relationship with their customers. Interpersonal relationships between company sales employees and customer supply chain procurement is a given.

But what about including president to president, and officer to officer? Leading from the front lines connects management, customers, and employees.

Business relationships are never perfect. There are very few companies operating with 100% product fulfillment, product quality, or customer service. When companies can't get it right with their largest customers, how do B and C customer fare?

Top management should be refining customer expectations at every opportunity. What business defined as expectations yesterday is not acceptable today. The real fact is owners and officers should be engaged with customers. Customer engagement is not something to delegate because of company departmental silo's.

Departmental Silo's

Departmental silo's tend to hide challenges rather than resolve them. The victim is the customer. The larger the company becomes, the more complex the structure of its departmental silo's. Company departments are sometimes territorial, predatory, and resistant to improvement. They align to symptoms rather than the sources of challenge.

The other challenge to consider is employee attrition. When employees leave the company, so does the relationship. If the employee is toxic, then it's probably good. But when a quality employee leaves the company doubt builds. Single source customer relationships contribute to loss of trust and confidence in the company. Excessive employee turnover invites scrutiny and competitive review.

The Price Myth

The notion that most customers leave because of price is myth. The real reason a significant number of customers leave is because of poor company communication and business practices. If a quality relationship existed with the customer, resolution could have occurred.

Effective leadership manages the customer relationship. It listens, becomes involved, and resolves customer challenges. It assumes nothing. Challenges instead become transparent and are everyone's issue, not one department.

Pivot Your Thinking

What if executive and management compensation incentives were tied to customer satisfaction and loyalty? How satisfied would customers become? How would customer loyalty be influenced? How could market share and competitive advantage be maximized?

The real truth is some management teams have forgotten about customer retention, penetration, and innovation. Key management quit doing what made them successful. In the beginning the business started out in a small office or a garage. The customer came first no matter what.

Nothing has fundamentally changed; interpersonal customer relationships are the heart and soul of business sustainability. As companies grow, top management becomes isolated from customers. Other duties have taken priority over customer relations.

Relevancy

There are relevant companies and those becoming irrelevant. Relevant companies realize effective customer relationships and best practices set the stage for healthy discussion. Quality customer relationships open the door for collaborative innovation and greater perceived value.

Non-relevant companies are losing out to competitors. If they expect to retain customer satisfaction and future transactions, interpersonal communication is critical. If they expect to innovate, customer collaboration is imperative. Non relevant companies face a slow slide because they fail to value customer relationships.

Customer Attrition

What is your customer attrition rate? Normal attrition for your industry might be two to three percentage points. Every percentage lost above normal attrition is a sign of company and customer challenges.

Any loss greater than two to three percentage points should cause alarm. The leadership team should investigate the real reasons for customer attrition.

Too Big to Fail

Thinking your company is too big to fail? For the record, there is a list of large publicly traded companies failing to meet growth expectations. The days of relying on acquisition for growth, as compared to organic growth, is a systemic risk. It's also evidence of flawed leadership.

Financial buyers of business should certainly review inefficiencies and work to improve them. But they should also place strategic value on the people and best practices that made a brand successful. They should work to retain those qualities. The culture is the brand. Without culture the brand ceases to deliver value.

Would it surprise you to learn many high-quality customers communicate a different perspective on supplier quality? These customers have a high awareness of "Organizational

Quality" from suppliers because they contribute to greater profit margins.

These customers realize exceptional suppliers provide goods and services with less internal dysfunction and expense. The fact is exceptional suppliers consistently provide superior goods and services nearly 100% of the time.

"Respectfully, to suppliers not approaching the 100% level, you don't know, what you don't know."

Organizational Quality

Organizational Quality is focused on effective management leadership, healthy cultures, and sound strategies of the entire organization. Customers expect superior relationships, consistent communication, and timely challenge resolution. They expect innovation for new income streams.

Is your business adapting fast enough to survive?

If a supplier isn't delivering organizational quality, they're simply irrelevant in today's business environment.

Average is Inconsistent Performance

Average is an acceptable performance level for many companies and employee ratings. What average really means is inconsistent performance. Average is the result of blending the highs and lows. The highs are great, and the lows are inconsistent performance. Everyone remembers the lows.

What we often find is the vast majority of companies rate their employees as average. Inconsistency means both management and employee performance varies from day to day.

Employees in average companies often rate their management as average.

Leadership and management practices vary from situation to situation. Quality communication varies from day to day. This also means strategies and objectives are inconsistently achieved. Customer satisfaction varies from order to order.

Average and inconsistency creates an environment of chaos and dysfunction. Financial management, risk management, and sustainability are influenced by average performance.

Concepts to Ponder

1. What percentage of employees in the organization are rated as average?
2. Do departmental silo's in the organization influence employee performance and customer satisfaction?
3. Is the organization approach strategic or chaos oriented?

Article 15

Customer Perspective

Customers realize quality suppliers don't magically happen. It's a result of supplier management and employees effectively performing their jobs.

Customers expect engaged relationships and communication from suppliers. They expect 100% order, fill, and ship metrics with every transaction. They expect the product quality or service quality to consistently meet specifications. Finally, they expect innovation from suppliers to remain relevant.

Customers are realistic. It's not a perfect world in manufacturing or service. It's how the supplier manages their challenges which make the difference.

Customers expect corrective action when product or service levels go off course. Customers expect a positive outcome despite "occasional" adversity. The operational word here is occasional. Ultimately customer satisfaction through each transaction determines customer loyalty. This is competitive advantage.

Organizational quality doesn't cost, it pays.

High quality customers realize you get what you pay for. Low price often means challenged organizational quality along with inconsistent products and communication.

These customers have learned through experience, it's better to pay a fair price and receive predictable value.

Customer Attrition

Quality customers choose gold standard suppliers because they consistently perform as quality organizations. Gold standard suppliers are focused on key performance indicators (KPI's).

These KPI's benchmark performance metrics of management, sales, operations, production, distribution, and other departments.

Price is often simply an excuse by customers to eliminate poor performance.

Average and inconsistent companies seem to attract average and inconsistent customers. As a result, profit margins, innovation, and growth are average and inconsistent. Self-inflicted, the business devalues itself.

Contrary to some, customer attrition is often a consequence of average and poor performance, not price.

Customer relationships generally flourish with suppliers who are engaged with their business. High-capacity suppliers deliver both quality relationships and deliverables.

The mantra of superior organizational quality is 100% performance from top to bottom. When customer attrition exceeds the ability of the sales department to replenish the customer base, sales growth declines.

The leaky bucket metaphor is a result of primary management inconsistency, not sales. For example, management can add its customer attrition values to sales goals and determine what the true growth rate needs to be.

If customer attrition is 5% and the company growth expectation is 5%, sales needs to grow at 10%. So, managing customer retention should be a top priority for management at all levels.

From a customer perspective, inconsistency means the supplier is unpredictable and potentially toxic. It's toxic because quality customers recognize average contaminates their organization.

Customer supply chains filled with dysfunctional suppliers creates internal havoc. Internally, customers experience employee burnout from toxic suppliers. Respectfully, it's difficult to defend an 80% order, fill, and ship rate to a quality customer.

Supplier Culture

Customers evaluate their supplier culture. Supplier perception is reality. Supplier culture is based on employee perception, not management. Reality is culture is transmitted to customers via their purchase transactions.

Internally, average performance is a primary contributor to toxic cultures. This toxicity breeds through poor communication and expectations from both management and unhappy employees.

I always find it interesting when an average company makes a high-performance hire. Frequently in the course of 6 months, the high-performance employee is performing at average levels, or has found a different employer out of frustration.

Perception is reality. Employees communicate culture with every transaction.

High-capacity managers and employees value culture. 360° Organizational Assessments benchmark cultural quality. Assessments allow management to maintain a top-to-top relationship with all employees. Simply stated, effective leaders recognize culture management delivers tremendous value.

Leadership - The 80/20 Performance Rule

Sales revenue is a result. Customer loyalty is a result. Effective goals, strategies, and tactics are a result. Most importantly, execution and accountability is a result of quality leadership.

Equal accountability means everyone in the organization is held equally accountable. If average and inconsistent is the expectation, that's what happens. If the benchmark is greater than average, that's what happens.

Does the common 80/20 rule apply to your organization? That is, where 20% of the employees consistently achieve 80% of the objectives.

What is the financial burden of 80% of employees not consistently achieving objectives?

Whatever the ratio is for your business, there are financial liabilities for poor performance.

Innovation - Remaining Customer Relevant

Superior leadership, healthy cultures, and effective strategies allow enterprises to focus resources on innovation. Rather than constantly being in firefighting mode, they are able to collaborate with customers on new goods and services.

> *Innovation allows suppliers to collaborate and build relationships with customers.*

New income streams build company financial stability. Innovation adds to the value customers expect.

The Technology Conundrum

Technology is a platform to collect, store, organize, and communicate information. Production facilities use robotics for task-based functions. Technology drives your car. And your phone is an information and communication resource that can direct you to drive off a cliff.

> *Technology can help companies become more efficient. But not necessarily more effective.*

Technology effectiveness is determined by the quality of management and employees contributing, interpreting, analyzing, and communicating information. Average performance companies are generally average in technology effectiveness.

Quality leadership, culture, and strategy creates effective technology. There are many companies spending 2-3% of their resources yearly on technology. What if the some of this investment shifted to developing their human resources?

Concepts to Ponder

1. How does the organization measure customer attrition and why?
2. What performance rating would top customers to your organization provide if asked?
3. What level of customer satisfaction is enhanced and delivered from the company's customer service department?

Section 3
Culture Management and Organizational Structure

Consider these remarkable facts influencing culture management.

- **Financial Losses Due to Cultural Challenges** – US$288 billion dollars. "One in five Americans has left a job in the past five years due to bad company culture."[5]

- **Employee Turnover** – 58 percent of those who left a job because of workplace culture cited their manager as the reason behind their decision.[6]

- **Employee Attrition** – Separations indicated a high of 60.5% attrition in Retail/Wholesale and 11.8% in Energy. Data provided is the number of voluntary, involuntary, and retirement separations in 2017.[7]

History – A Catalyst for Change

History tends to cycle. If you are a student of history, consider the Industrial Revolutions that changed the world. Each Industrial Revolution contributed to a cultural

---

[5] Source: Society for Human Resource Management

[6] Source: Society for Human Resource Management
[7] Source: US Turnover Survey of 163 U.S. organizations

revolution. While today's empire builders offer unique vision, they were not the first.

1. The First Industrial Revolution used steam power to create mass production. Years (1790-1840) [8]

2. The Second Industrial Revolution used electric power to advance mass production. 19th century [9]

3. The Third Industrial Revolution is using technology to automate mass production. 20th century [10]

4. The Fourth Industrial Revolution is using technology to connect the physical, digital, and biological. [11]

5. The Fifth Industrial Revolution is aligned toward automation through artificial intelligence (AI).

Interestingly, many industries are still engaged in the evolution of the third and fourth Industrial Revolutions. As a result, their cultures are evolving to fit the appropriate revolution. Depending on where your business exists in its relationship to the industrial revolution, leadership must evolve as well.

---

[8] Source: Desoutter Tools
[9] Source: Desoutter Tools
[10] Source: Desoutter Tools
[11] Source: Desoutter Tools

One common response often stated is that the technology revolution is different from other revolutions. In some cases, this may be true, but immigration, migration, wars, diversity, equal opportunity, political change, and innovation all influenced the decisions of each prior revolution.

Leadership from technology companies see their products as the lifeblood of all industry. Leadership from many other industries see technology as a tool to manage information and tasks.

Industry has had email, text, telephone, computer reporting, and all the other components of the technological revolution for years. Today AI is set to modify humanity.

Economists and private equity have created every imaginable metric possible to measure success or failure. Ultimately, quality leadership is the single best forecaster of short- and long-term financial success.

In my view, interpersonal communication remains the greatest challenge to business and society. It's about people and no amount of machine learning or artificial intelligence can alter humanity.

Article 16

Organizational Quality

Every business has challenges. Most challenges have solutions, and some do not. As managers and leaders, it's important to reflect on the good, bad, and ugly components of your business.

These are challenging times for many companies. When you're in the middle of battle day after day, we become hardened to dysfunction and chaos.

Eventually we become accepting of chaos. We also become accepting of stress and emotional baggage tagging along with chaos.

Devil is in the Details

Consider this, sales revenue is a result. Customer loyalty is a result. Profit margins are a result. Each depends on effective management leadership, culture, and strategy to achieve success.

The wildcard in all of this is the quality of the organization. Quality organizations understand the "devil is in the details." Most often it's the lack of management attention or understanding to the details creating chaos and dysfunction.

What's so interesting for many companies is assessing customer and employee retention. So often, high quality customers and employees don't leave because of price or compensation. They leave because of organizational quality.

Tweaking Your Management Approach

Effective management systems work to accomplish the details. Communication, best practices, and expectations follow a prescribed course. We have learned big course corrections are generally not helpful.

Small and steady course corrections allow the business, management, and employees to adjust to the system's approach. Chaos and dysfunctional behaviors lessen. Customer transactions and relationships improve.

Systems tend to take the emotion out of business and relationships. Systems deal with facts.

Facilitators

Business systems allow management to become facilitators of leadership, culture and strategy. That is, managers are able to focus on opportunity, rather than achieve tasks.

Employees are able to achieve their job function. Strategies and objectives are better executed.

Stress and burnout are no longer a daily event. Organizational quality becomes the objective of facilitators.

System Results

What we observe is sales revenue, customer loyalty, and profitability improve. As organizational quality improves, so does performance. Both satisfy customers and employees.

Success comes one step at a time. Management discussion, collaboration, and accountability make systems successful. Everyone works within the system.

Management teams learning together exposes the good, bad, and ugly. Management teams' problem solving together creates solutions and sustainability. Chaos and dysfunction become infrequent events.

Concepts to Ponder

1. Does the organization effectively identify chaos managers and business practices?
2. Is the company accepting of chaos as an everyday occurrence?
3. Does the organization utilize management systems to equip all managers with tools and resources?

Article 17

What is a Business System?

Business systems are a model to consistently and predictably achieve quality results. Systems are structures. Like a building, the system supports the foundation, walls, and roof. Structure is a set of process and performance boundaries both management and employees work within during the course of business.

Externally, business systems allow management to focus on growing and delivering greater value to customers. Competitive advantage is the driver of greater revenue and profitability.

Internally, business systems allow management to focus on employee achievement, retention, and loyalty. All of which are driven by the quality of leadership, culture, and strategy.

Leaders proactively manage and achieve objectives. Managers manage activities and tasks. There is a difference.

The capacity of the enterprise is limited by the capacity of its management team. If a management team is unskilled or overwhelmed, the business fails to grow.

Business systems allow management to become better decision makers and leaders. Enterprise capacity expands as the system establishes and supports sustainable performance results.

Unfortunately, the vast majority of managers spend their time resolving crisis situations. Most are symptoms and not the true source of crisis. Many times, these situations should have been resolved long ago, and continue to re-establish themselves. Sometimes on a daily basis.

The result of a management systems approach is customers receive superior quality, service, and value. That is, customers receive consistent and predictable deliverables and behavior from the company.

The second result of a management systems approach is employees receive and work in a quality environment of team, job security, and fair compensation.

The final outcome is the company gains competitive advantage through consistent employee trust and customer relationships.

Culture Management Systems

The vast majority of business managers measure cultural health by gut feeling and emotion. If it's a good day, cultural health is fine. If it's a bad day, cultural health becomes negative.

Perception is defined by feelings. Company culture is a function of employee perception. We measure employee perception in 10 actionable areas.

Cultural health influences nearly every aspect of an organization. It's a primary reason objectives are consistently achieved, and employees retained. When customer and employee retention rates are poor, it's a clear indicator employee culture is challenged.

Interesting enough, challenged cultures are generally activity based. Quality cultures are generally more objective based. Ultimately for activity-based organizations, the churn of customers and employees leaving the company set the stage for toxic cultures.

Cultural health isn't just about salaries and benefits. People want to work for an organization that places value in a TEAM dynamic, job security, and fair and equal compensation.

People have pride, loyalty, and want to earn a sense of accomplishment. The fact remains most people leave a job not because of the work, but rather because of their manager.

Culture management systems allow management to benchmark and improve the source of cultural challenges rather than the symptoms. This allows leaders to solve sources of challenges rather than managers solving symptoms.

Weak or toxic cultures influence enterprise capacity. Employees are assets influencing revenue and profitability. When we identify challenges and opportunities in culture, it takes leadership to make course corrections.

Strategic Systems

Revenue and profitability are a result, not an objective. Well-conceived strategies are concerned with opportunity, risk, and return.

Strategy is not how to do something. Rather, strategy

discovers whether we should, or should not, engage the objective.

The devil is in the details before a strategy is initiated. Effective Strategic Systems discover prior to implementation if the risk, return, or the investment is too great.

Effective leaders rely on a Strategic System to establish a decision-making model. The system model educates the team on process and establishes performance boundaries.

Highly successful companies develop strategies, align the tactics, and communicate the message the same way every time. There's no random occurrence.

Quality strategy defines the strength and value of management leadership. It builds trust and respect with the TEAM and customers.

Competitive Advantage

Business Systems create high performance organizations. They allow organizations to grow without loss of control or wandering outside their core values.

Customers expect 100% quality, service, and value. Employees expect 100% TEAM, job security, fair compensation.

When customers and employees connect at the 100% level, that's competitive advantage. The result is greater revenue and profitability.

Concepts to Ponder

1. How does your organization measure total quality?
2. How close is your organization to 100% in quality, service, and value?
3. What is your closest competitor doing with regard to total quality that your organization is not?

Article 18

Embracing Your Cultural Health"

Unfortunately, a magic elixir for improving cultural challenges simply does not exist. Every customer transaction is impacted by the quality of organizational culture. And every employee has established cultural perception that they communicate to customers.

Embracing Your Cultural Health

Cultural health is based on employee and management perception. Perception is what people feel. Perception drives brands. Perception drives cultural health. Perception drives employee behavior and business practices. Perception drives trust. Perception drives customer satisfaction and eventually, loyalty. Perception drives profit.

Management establishes and cultivates the boundaries of cultural health. Management is the fulcrum of brand perception. If management fails to understand its perception, how can they understand employee and customer expectations?

Perception is reality. Perception guides our decisions and narrative. What managers perceive is their decision-making reality. And what employees perceive is their reality. Their perception influences employee retention and productivity.

Perception is transactional. Employees communicate perception to customers with every transaction. Employees at every level are ambassadors of company perception and culture.

Quality leaders understand and value perception because it establishes conditions and boundaries for excellence. It causes us to investigate, forge ahead, and examine the facts.

Facts and truth are not always the same. Sometimes we place our faith in the wrong people and practices.

Pivot Your Thinking

Companies with poor cultural health eventually become irrelevant to shareholders as failed investments. As for employees, they move to another job. Competitors and other industries poach valuable employees. Management struggles to achieve its goals.

The fact is organizations with high-quality cultures consistently deliver greater quality, service, innovation, and shareholder value. In this environment, employee retention is greater and collaborative relationships thrive between customers and employees.

Key Contributors to Cultural Health

- <u>Leadership</u> - Leadership is influenced and influences cultural health. A quality culture allows management to consistently achieve objectives. Superior employee perception of management is an indicator of effective communication.
- <u>Culture Management</u> – Culture management allows leaders to understand cultural challenges using facts and evidence rather than emotion or assumption. A well-defined Culture Management program sets

boundaries and expectations for growing cultural health.
- <u>Effective Planning</u> – Employees and customers both expect planning, consistency, and execution of objectives. Companies failing to effectively plan and execute find themselves on an endless loop of customer and employee attrition. Their view is why stick with an organization failing to deliver on its promises?

What is My Cultural Health?

Assessing your company's cultural health is the first step in understanding its cultural challenges. The 360° Organizational Assessment process benchmarks measurable facts rather than subjective assumptions. Our assessment process for example identifies ten (10) areas of greatest cultural concern.

The most important concept to grasp regarding the 360° Cultural Assessment process is it functions as an important tool. It identifies the difference between source and symptom. The fact is most managers solve symptoms, not the source of its challenges.

The 360° Organizational Assessment process is an excellent indicator of why financial growth is inconsistent or stagnant. The failure of management to execute strategies and tactics is a primary source of employee and customer attrition.

The 360° Organizational Assessment KPIs (key performance indicators), provide a roadmap for improvement. Cultural change is not a quick fix. It requires commitment, engagement, and accountability.

Concepts to Ponder

1. How does your organization measure cultural health?
2. What is the expectation of cultural health?
3. Does your organization equate its financial success to its cultural health?

Article 19

Improving Challenged Cultures: Cultural Management System

There is simply no Silver Bullet for people-related challenges. Every customer transaction is impacted by the quality of the organization. But keep in mind our dialogue is not about basic business mechanics; it's about communication and the quality of our customers and employees.

> Sam Walton said, "There is only one boss. The customer. And he can fire everybody in the company from the chairman on down, simply by spending his money somewhere else."

The fact is that challenged cultures generally result in poor customer satisfaction and unpredictable company growth. That said, those in leadership positions possess the power to create positive change in an organization suffering from a negative culture.

Company managers generally operate as gatekeepers. Gatekeepers govern and influence business practices, and the intellectual and behavioral performance of subordinates.

To improve culture takes an understanding of the importance of culture, an honest assessment of current organizational culture, and a strategic path for improvement.

Pivot Your Thinking

Low unemployment rates have added another component to management. Employees are exercising their right to a quality team environment, job security, and fair wages and benefits.

With low employment rates across the country, quality employees are quietly writing their own ticket with new employers that offer better opportunities. But understand, these opportunities are not just about compensation; rather they are about the quality of the organization.

As leaders, we must distinguish the difference between quality, value, and price. Our best customers generally recognize the value of a superior organization.

The Cultural Management System

For our clients, Tacticware conducts 360° Organizational Assessments as a way to measure health and stability of the organization. Our assessments are designed to benchmark the culture of an organization through true understanding of employee perception and customer satisfaction.

What we have found interesting is the fact that often, both customers and employees share similar views about the perception of the company. Facts and evidence typically line up regarding organizational quality and dysfunction.

We consult with clients nationwide, spanning industries, enterprise verticals, and employee counts. What we have found in measuring quantifiable perception results is this: low scores in employee perception (culture) generally reflect low scores in customer satisfaction.

Consider these Customer and Employee Satisfaction Expectations.

Figure 1 - Top 5 Employee Satisfactions Expectations

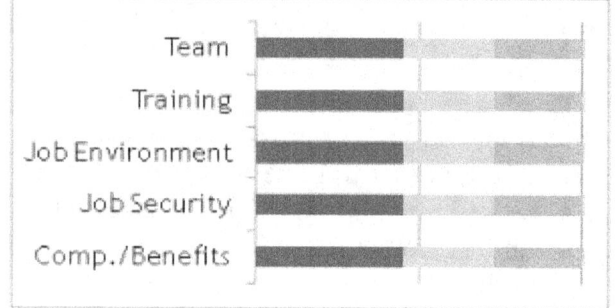

Figure 2 - Top 5 Customer Satisfaction Expectations

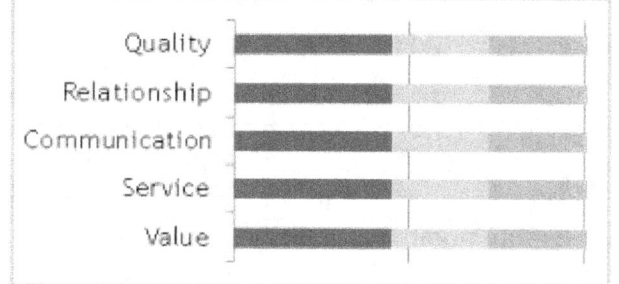

The Importance of Quality Management

The research we have seen shows this as a simple truth: organizations must retain quality management and employees if the enterprise expects to gain competitive advantage.

If we are to improve customer quality, we must also demonstrate continuous improvement of company culture.

Consider these interesting comparisons found within surveys regarding customer and employee perception:

- Customer Surveys Report: Oftentimes, customers leave not because of price, but because of company business practices.

- Employee Assessments Report: Oftentimes, employees leave not because of compensation, but because of company business practices.

We suggest effective company culture must be a managed discipline. That is, company culture should be managed with the same scrutiny and importance as financial and legal affairs. Company culture is the real source of brand success and superior financial results.

The real truth is many management teams don't understand culture or its value to the bottom line. Culture management moves from vague subjective indicators to quantitative results. The final result is increased revenue and profitability.

Throughout this Article, we introduce questions you should honestly ask yourself to determine the true state of your organization. We often see that when a company encounters difficulty, some of the problems can be traced back to leadership, and most importantly the source, which is culture.

Actionable Suggestions

Please consider the following:

- Is company culture consistently evaluated? How frequently?
- Are company vision, mission, and core values established and consistently enforced by management?
- Does the company have a current Employee Handbook? Is it equally enforced by all management?
- Does the company, if applicable, have a Safety Handbook? Is it equally enforced by all management?

Our Definition of Organizational Culture

"Organizational Culture is a system of shared values, beliefs, and business practices."- Investopedia

The Cultural Management System governs how people behave, communicate, plan, engage, and perform within the organization. Company vision, mission, and core values establish cultural expectations.

Leadership is responsible for effectively managing the Cultural System.

Successful Companies Enforce the System

Successful companies consistently promote and enforce Core Values. Management effectively introduces company values to new employees via on-boarding processes.

Management also consistently reinforces company values to existing employees. In a successful culture, these values are posted in every hall, gathering place, break room, and warehouse. They are discussed in major meetings and discussions.

The reason is clear: Culture is Your Brand.

Another action demonstrated by successful companies is that primary and secondary management are directly accountable for the organization's cultural compliance. Cultural transparency is clear if we open our eyes. In a successful company, offenders are required to either improve through a performance plan or be replaced.

As a result, successful companies spend less time cleaning up disasters and engaged in crisis management. After all, a significant number of disasters are created by cultural rebels.

Effective leaders instead spend more time with performance achievers and innovation. As such, customer collaboration and relationships are enriched resulting in greater customer retention.

But here's the thing, company Vision, Mission, and Core Values must be realistic and practical. Leadership must consistently enforce all values equally. If not, credibility is lost with employees and customers.

Actionable Suggestions

Honestly ask yourself and your team the following questions.

- Review your company vision, mission, and core values. Do they accurately reflect company direction and expectations?
- Consider the last large customer or quality employee the company failed to retain. What was the real reason?
- Does your company have current job descriptions defining primary and secondary objective expectations and associated responsibilities?
- Does your company train all levels of management regarding affirmative defenses against litigation regarding discrimination, harassment, medical leave, and workplace violence?
- Is the company environment safe, secure, and professional?

Cultural Rebels

Cultural rebels are ambassadors of company culture. Unfortunately, they don't share the values of the company. Poor performance, communication deficiencies, and behavioral challenges are part of the rebel makeup.

Rebels spread dysfunction and mayhem throughout the company with their business practices. Employees and customers experience it. Customers who have had enough dysfunction find other suppliers.

In fact, some rebels work hard to minimize leadership effectiveness. Sometimes management members are really rebel leaders, toxic to cultural improvement.

Rebels generally don't have negative intent. They like how things are and discourage cultural change. Sometimes they fail to understand market conditions and competitive threat.

The moment company leadership takes their eye from the ball; rebels push culture back to its original state.

Quality leadership in every department matters. Quality employees in every department matters. Again, quality employees sometimes leave not because of compensation, but because of company business practices.

Financially, rebels create significant financial risk. When we consider the true cost of rebel overhead in labor dollars and the extended liability to productivity, customer satisfaction, and management time it becomes very expensive.

The 80/20 rule generally applies. 80% of the revenue is generate by 20% of the team. The financial consequences become dramatic when one multiplies out the risk.

Actionable Suggestions

Consider the following questions honestly.

- What is the hard dollar cost of each employee classification in the organization?
- What are the percentages of employees consistently meeting expectations and those who are inconsistent?
- Determine how rebels influence your team with these thoughts.
- What is the level of pushback by management and employees on new ideas and innovation in your organization?
- Is there a general failure to achieve assigned objectives?
- What level of negative customer feedback exists?

- Is there a failure by employees to complete all duties?
- What negative attitudes and behaviors tend to influence team performance?

Unequal Accountability

Managers who permit unequal accountability break the Cultural Management System.

We define Unequal Accountability as "management holding like employees accountable for differing job and behavioral expectations."

Did you know? – The number one employee complaint isn't compensation, rather its unequal accountability by management.

Leaders allowing poor performance by rebels eventually influence quality employees to lower their performance efforts. In our cultural reviews, many employees have responded with, "Why should I work so hard when other don't?"

Rebels create the lowest-performance denominator. They set the bar of dysfunction with customers and establish perception. Company leadership not confronting rebel performance condones this negative behavior.

The Rebel Virus is an infectious disease. This virus nullifies the best efforts and business practices of the organization. Essentially, the virus limits the capacity of the organization.

Actionable Suggestions

- Consider the question "Are all employees treated equally, or do favorites exist?" Review this helpful list to help determine the answer.
- Do rebels have a Performance Improvement Plan in place to correct deficiencies?
- Does management end up completing work rebels should have completed?
- Does the organization consistently meet its operational and financial goals?
- Do strategic plans generally succeed or fail?
- Does secondary management enforce best practices equally with all employees?

Effective Leadership is the Antidote

Today, leadership has every imaginable software tool available to manage performance. For example, ERP software (Enterprise Resource Planning) manages supply chain, production, and operations; CRM (Customer Resource Planning) manages customer intelligence and sales metrics; and financial software manages receivables, liabilities, and potential risk.

Despite all these software tools and resources, rebels still evade and game the system. The real challenge is Leadership.

Imagine if you will for a moment:

- Who is an example of your single best manager and employee?
- Who consistently delivers objectives, is self-managed, and reflects the vision, mission, and core values of the company?

- Then imagine if all managers and employees performed their jobs with these skills.
- What if leaders focused on culture as a discipline?

Frankly, leadership is the source of most cultural challenges. The real question is why would a customer want to purchase from your business?

Most of this answer is derived from the Top 5 Customer Satisfaction results.

- Quality
- Relationships
- Service
- Innovation
- Price/Value

Notice that price/value is last at #5. New and higher quality customers assess their perception of a total quality organization - not just price.

Actionable Suggestions

Hope for the best and plan for the worst.

- Identify managers who understand and demonstrate the value of culture and brand.
- Utilize use insurance and legal professionals for specific support and training to understand the liability of improperly managed employee terminations.

Adaption

The ability of a business to adapt and prosper when confronted by adversity, competitors, and market conditions is centered in culture.

Culture is a managed discipline and should be met with the same scrutiny and importance as financial and legal affairs. Company culture is the real source of brand success and superior financial results. After all, "Culture is the Company Brand."

Companies with strong cultures are proactive innovators. Employees are self-managed and achieve objectives. They respect and embrace the vision, mission, and core values. Most importantly, quality customers recognize the value of total quality because the results are predictable.

Concepts to Ponder

1. Is your organization adapting to cultural change?
2. Is unequal accountability a common practice in the organization?
3. Does senior management measure success based on cultural health?

Article 20

Shareholder Value, It's About People

In this Article, we discuss three cultural types often found in business: Price-Based, Production, and Customer-Centric cultures. Each environment affects revenue, client retention, and shareholder value.

Additionally, we discuss how to analyze your company culture and begin to embrace cultural change.

Introduction

Is there a magic strategy for increasing shareholder value?

From our perspective, quality and self-managed people are the magic. It's a blend of positive culture and effective strategy, achieved by skilled people.

Companies with keen innovation and a growing customer base demonstrate a successful culture. They retain productive, self-managed leaders and employees. The result is achievement of plans, and, of course, shareholder value.

Self-managed leaders and employees generate their own success. They are productive, profitable, and effective. Given a goal they achieve it with little fanfare.

Self-management means the ability to plan, schedule, execute, and report achievement with little supervision.

Collaboration and enthusiasm both become contagious. They spill over into customers and community.

Positive culture creates an environment of achievement. Employees and customers are beneficiaries of best practices. Shareholders are recipients of increased earnings.

Strategy execution is influenced by company culture. The failure to consistently execute strategies and objectives is a result of flawed company culture. Culture is derived from the company vision, mission, and core values. It's the foundation of productivity, retention, and growth.

Consider this: culture allows the enterprise to achieve its potential.

It is a choice as to which customers and revenue sources we pursue. Customer choice is a result of culture. Quality customers have behaviors and expectations regarding products, service, and business practices.

Good customers embrace collaboration and innovation. Less-than-stellar customers have the opposite effect.

We generally find three cultural types in industry.

- Price-Based
- Production
- Customer-Centric

Each environment is unique but can be changed if necessary. Let us begin first with Price-Based Cultures.

Price-Based Cultures

Companies that are focused on low price have a corresponding culture. It creates a commodity mentality; it's a constant race to the pricing floor.

The commodity mentality infects management and employees. Since low price customers are the easiest to sell, entire companies develop a level of comfort with the price-conscious customer. Over time, the vast majority of customers become commodity purchasers and revenue is stagnant.

Price-based cultures occur when management, sales, and operational teams limit the value that they bring to the customer. They fail to effectively manage customer relationships, service, and business practices.

Quality customers expect quality, service, and business practices to meet specific expectations. Many times, companies lose business with great customers not because of price, but because of business practices.

Companies with large volume customers purchasing at low margins complicate the challenge. Customers leverage the manufacturer over price. Customer loyalty is dictated by price rather than quality. The company is trapped in a vicious circle.

Production Cultures

Companies focused on supplying high-quality products generally create loyal customers. Equipment, manufacturing processes, and supply chain are top-notch.

Legacy customers receive quality products at a fair price. The challenge is new customers become more difficult to secure because the market has evolved.

Often times, company culture is centered on production because it's tangible and logical. Margins, capacity, and purchases are highly managed. The conundrum is to eliminate less profitable business from the portfolio rather than expand production. It's a sound business model until the enterprise begins to turn quality customers away.

Some companies find the transition to finding new growth daunting. Growth strategies are challenging because people, communication, and relationships are intangible and fall outside the production comfort zone.

Sometimes sales teams lose their edge and relationships from years of saying no. Failure to achieve growth happens when the company fails to modify its approach to its people and customer relationships.

Often, we find innovation is limited by the capacity of the management team. Market intelligence isn't valued or used wisely. Growth strategies are a broad-brush stroke rather than specific and calculating. Competitors with greater emphasis on quality people and customer collaboration tend to gain market share.

Quality customers are managing risk better today than ever. They want it all. They trust and are loyal to suppliers with superior quality, people, service, and business practices. It's simply more profitable.

Customer-Centric Cultures

Companies embracing a "Customer-Centric Culture" live differently. They have a collaborative relationship with customers, management, and employees. The difference is communication, accountability, and achievement. All parties are striving for achievement.

Interestingly, a customer-centric culture eventually broadens from simply sales to include operations, R/D, administration, and production. The fact is that customers establish perception about the company from its total picture rather than just sales. This perception establishes trust and customer satisfaction when all pieces are working together in a positive way.

Customer-centric enterprises create positive employee perception. Employee perception is an indicator of customer perception. It's transmitted in every communication and delivery. Oftentimes customer and employee retention aligns with perception. Create a positive employee environment and it will influence customer purchases.

Organizations with superior product quality, people, service, and business practices seek out the greater opportunities. Growth strategies are more effective because objectives are achieved rather than tasks.

Ultimately, this culture becomes a "Field of Dreams" when customers seek out the best in all categories.

Customer Expectations

Quality customers understand the value of culture and quality. Ask them. In fact, quality customers measure key components of supplier quality. They set expectations and boundaries for trust.

Why purchase from or collaborate with a supplier who fails expectations? They want to collaborate and purchase from leaders and innovators.

We sometimes learn from a company that they lost a customer due to price. Further investigation often reveals price was not the culprit. Many times, the challenge is a result of the company failing to communicate value or effectively manage a relationship.

Quality customers are focused on risk management. Purchasing from companies with flawed cultures and less-than-stellar performance is a risk. Poor quality and service are a liability.

Tip: Measuring customer satisfaction provides great insight into better understanding company culture.

What's My Culture?

Benchmarking your company culture is the first step to increasing shareholder value. The 360° Organizational Assessment identifies areas of opportunity. An assessment is an excellent indicator of why enterprise growth and attrition could be challenged in your organization.

After one understands the cultural key indicators, plans can be made for improvement. That said, cultural change is not a quick fix. It requires commitment, engagement, and accountability.

Concepts to Ponder

1. How would you rate company culture based on employee perception?
2. How would you rate company culture based on management's perception?
3. Is your company a price-based, production, or customer-centric culture?

Article 21

Disrupters to Sales Revenue, The Impact of Leadership and Culture Management

Customers are perceptive of supplier flaws. They recognize suppliers with consistent performance are predictable contributors to their financial health.

It's pretty simple; when customers don't trust suppliers, they limit exposure. Why trust a company or salesperson who fails to deliver? Leadership and cultural challenges eventually impact customer retention.

Pivot Your Thinking

Leadership and company culture determine brand value. Effective leadership is constantly verifying and enforcing company culture and customer satisfaction standards.

Effective leaders focus on top-to-top customer relationships in addition to sales department staff.

> *The fact is leaders and companies can't code their way to strategic customer relationships. They can code their way to efficiencies.*

Personal visits, phone calls, and emails from senior leadership to customers send a message of commitment and trust.

Disruptors of Customer Satisfaction

Effective leaders consistently verify compliance of these Customer Satisfaction Conditions. When company culture is aligned to these conditions the company becomes a preferred supplier.

Disruption to sales revenue growth occurs when these conditions are not top of mind by leadership.

1. <u>Quality</u>: products/service exactly as promised
2. <u>Relationships</u>: consistent and professional relationships
3. <u>Service</u>: timely, actionable, and friendly solutions resolving challenges
4. <u>Innovation</u>: true innovation that contributes to growth
5. <u>Value</u>: fair and predictable pricing

So many times, we hear clients have lost a strategic customer over price. After investigation we often find price is not responsible. It's company failure in customer satisfaction.

Questions:

1. Is company culture truly centered on customer satisfaction?
2. Does your company measure customer satisfaction?
3. What is the customer attrition rate?
4. What innovation has the company introduced in the last year?

Organizational Culture Definition

"Organizational Culture is a system of shared values, beliefs, and business practices." - Investopedia

The Cultural Management System governs how people behave, communicate, plan, engage, and perform within the organization. Company vision, mission, and core values establish cultural expectations.

Tip: Does company Vision and Mission Statements reflect the importance of customer satisfaction?

Growing Revenue, it's about Customer Perception

Excessive customer attrition has a profound impact on sales departments. Sometimes just as a new customer is on-boarded, an existing customer departs.

Customer retention is key to the financial stability of the company. It's the foundation of predictable revenue.

Consider this planning guide for understanding and managing customer attrition.

Sales Planning	Units	Percentage
(A) New period sales goal	106,000	106%
(B) Base period sales actual	100,000	100%
(C) Base units required to meet goal (A-B)	6,000	6.0%
(D) Projected customer attrition	8,000	8.0%
(E) Projected units to meet plan (C+D)	14,000	14.0%

- Line A is the new period sales goal of 106,000 units.
- Line B is last year sales of 100,000 units.
- Line C is a new sales goal of plus 6% or 6000 units.
- Line D is the customer attrition rate of 8% or 8000 units.
- Line E is the total of both sales growth of 6%, plus the attrition rate of 8%. To achieve plan, the company will require a total of 14%, or 14,000 units.

Often times companies fail to plan or manage for customer attrition. Even a single point improvement in customer attrition has dramatic impact on goals.

When we effectively manage disruptors to sales revenue growth, we also influence company culture.

Downstream Consequences

Companies embracing a "Customer Centric Culture" live differently. They have a collaborative relationship with customers, management, and employees. The difference is communication, accountability, and achievement. All parties are striving for achievement.

Sometimes companies experience excessive sales employee turnover because of toxic or poorly managed cultures. The fact is sales employees struggle to achieve goals when customers fail to trust the company.

What's My Culture?

Bench-marking your company culture is the first step in increasing revenue growth. The 360° Organizational Assessment identifies areas of opportunity. The assessment is an excellent indicator of why financial growth and attrition could be challenged in your organization.

After one understands cultural key indicators, plans can be made for improvement. Cultural change is not a quick fix. It requires commitment, engagement, and accountability.

Concepts to Ponder

1. Does management have a collaborative relationship with customers?
2. What is your customer attrition rate and why?
3. What are your disruptors of customer satisfaction?

Article 22

Culture Management - What We Don't Know, Does Hurt Us

Covid, and its variants, coupled with government responses have challenged management like no other calamity in recent history. And just when we think the business environment is improving, another challenge raises its ugly head.

The combination of employee attrition, supply chain inconsistencies, production challenges, and unpredictable revenue resurfaces to influence our business stability and personal lives. Then consider how all these factors work to influence customer perception.

Employee Perception- Did You Know?

Perception is our observation about a subject. Perception can be positive or negative. Positive employee perception is an indicator of positive cultural health. The greater the cultural health, the more likely the business will retain employees.

We can measure employee perception through 360° Organizational Assessments. Assessments allow management to benchmark and improve areas of greatest concern.

Dissatisfied employees respond to vulnerable cultures by low productivity or quitting. I suggest while some percentage of employees may say they are leaving over wages, the vast majority are leaving because of a toxic or non-rewarding work environment.

Challenged companies give them an obvious reason to leave. They seek better employment opportunities.

The true source of negative employee perception is often management challenges in leadership, communication, and business practices. Excessive attrition makes these challenges transparent.

Management teams should see these challenges as a great concern for the future. The primary question becomes, what is the <u>measured</u> employee perception of your business?

Cultural Health

Cultural health is based on employee perception. Employee perception is first determined by organizational quality. Organizational quality is based on company leadership, strategy, and business practices. It is not wages.

The following are five significant reasons to consider why employee perception is challenged.

Failure to Value Employees

Quality workers are the value of the company. They are an asset, not a liability. Treat them fairly. Compensate and bonus them fairly. Distribute workloads evenly. Communicate often and professionally.

Office Environment

Return to an office environment whenever possible. Employees resent having their personal and work lives overlap. And many employees struggle with the self-discipline necessary for balancing the work from home environment.

The vast majority of employees welcome and need social interaction. Sure, there are some who embrace isolation. But there are many employees living on the edge of a mental health crisis by constantly zooming from home. Set time boundaries on all conference meetings to minimize fatigue.

Employee Workload

The notion employees are achieving more at home than from the office is clever deception for most businesses. Those advocating this practice are naïve to the value of company culture. They simply do not understand the needs and wants of people. They lack understanding of employee expectations, productivity, training, and customer satisfaction.

Frankly, employees are resentful of working twelve or more hours a day, rather than the typical eight. Employees are mentally exhausted. Families are exhausted with the stress.

Managers piling more work on existing employee's even on a temporary basis, setting the stage for even greater resentment and attrition. Managers need to assess and prioritize employee workloads for value.

Failure to Communicate

Managers with poor communication skills fail to establish or develop trust and loyalty with employees. Employee satisfaction is critical to employee retention. Poor communication leads to strategic blunders and inconsistent best practices.

Employee accountability is a form of communication. When productivity and objective achievements decline, strategies fail. Employees recognize this condition as a ship without a rudder, and no career future for them.

Absence of Leadership

Challenged leadership and management practices create a toxic work environment. Why would existing or new employees want to stay with or engage with an employer who is culturally clueless?

Managers with poor approaches and business practices are a liability to business culture. Review attrition rates by department.

The fact is management failing to listen and address employee expectations is out of touch with their employee culture. And often, management failing to listen to their employees is probably out of touch with their customers as well.

Culturally driven companies will succeed in the future. Culturally challenged companies will no longer be relevant.

Culture is Everything

Believe it, employee culture is everything. Just ask your employees why they are staying or leaving. Employee culture connects your business to its goals and customers beyond a paycheck. Healthy cultures retain their employees. Unhealthy cultures have high employee attrition.

Most people need a job. Most people need steady income and benefits. Most people want to be loyal to their employer. Most people find job change extremely stressful.

Employee perception during the last two years has changed many companies. There has been a migration of unhappy employees to other businesses. Again, there are three generally accepted conditions for employee attrition. Respectively, they self- terminate because of:

1. Dissatisfaction with company business practices.
2. Dissatisfaction because of wages.
3. Some became entrepreneurs by starting their own business

In my view the greatest number of employees left because of dissatisfaction with their company, culture, and its business practices.

Concepts to Ponder

1. How would you rate the office environment of your organization?
2. In general, does management lead by example?
3. How would you assess the quality of communication in your business?

Article 23
Company Health Goes Beyond EBITA

EBITA, (earnings before interest, taxes, and amortization) is the primary measurement of business financial health. If a company isn't profitable, management cannot reinvest in future growth, innovation, reward shareholders, nor retain quality employees. One secret to EBITA growth lies in Culture Management.

EBITA isn't the only measurement of company health. Company health is also measured by the Cultural Assessment Index. That is, we measure employee, management, customer, and supplier perception. The perception of these group is the operating reality of the organization.

Consider this. EBITA is a <u>result</u> of goal achievement. Cultural health is a contributing <u>source</u> of goal achievement.

Positive cultural health is a combined result of quality leadership, culture management, and strategy. Cultural health reflects the financial capacity of the organization. While EBITA values change by quarter, cultural health is long term source of enterprise capacity.

Typical symptoms of a toxic culture generally include failure to achieve strategies and objectives, excessive employee attrition, customer attrition, inconsistent product, and service quality. Yes, some companies deliver acceptable EBITA values to shareholders despite their warts. They still produce satisfactory EBITA amid a toxic culture. They churn employees, customers, and management constantly. They make money in spite of themselves.

The question then, how much EBITA value did these companies lose over poor business practices?

Positive cultural perception contributes to superior customer relationships, innovation success, and gross margins. Improving your EBITA begins with improving your Cultural Index.

360 Organizational Assessment Index

We have found almost universally that employees, management, customers, and suppliers establish company perception based on the effectiveness of leadership, culture, strategy, and communication.

- Without leadership the company lacks boundaries and a true course.
- Without culture, teams fail to consistently achieve objectives.
- Without strategy, there is no plan and the company wanders.
- Without communication, people are not heard.

The Organizational Assessment Index measures ten (10) areas of perception. It establishes a direct line of communication from employees, management, customers, and suppliers to senior management. It identifies quantitatively why EBITA is challenged, and how to improve EBITA results.

360° Organizational Assessments- Identifying Trigger Points

Every company is different. Each have varying levels of leadership, cultural governance, and strategy. We identify the trigger points that are most impactful and actionable to our clients. While some enterprises may struggle with sales, others are struggling in service, logistics, or supply chain.

360° Organizational Assessments remove subjective interpretation by management. The facts are the facts. Sometimes management has an illusionary view of environment. And sometimes employees when asked about conditions by management will not truthfully communicate their perception

Final Thoughts

The Tacticware 360° Organizational Assessment identifies the cultural health of the business. The assessment is conducted on-line, and benchmarks employee perception. It assesses ten areas of greatest cultural concern.

EBITA. Without quality leadership, culture stagnates, customer value erodes, and attrition invades. The greater the Organizational Assessment Index ranking, the easier EBITA achievement becomes.

Concepts to Ponder

1. How would you rate the combined effectiveness of leadership, culture, strategy, and communication in your company?
2. What steps is your organization implementing to improve EBITDA?
3. What is the most destructive business practice your company delivers to employees?

Article 24
Revolutionize Your Culture, Culture Is Your Brand

If you were to ask a group of business professionals the definition of culture, you would likely receive a variety of responses. Sometimes they are right, other times they are not, as culture has impact on every facet of the organization and is felt in different ways.

Consider this definition:

> *Culture is the shared values and behaviors of its management and employees.*

Culture establishes perception, expectations, accountability, and performance. That culture is in turn transparent to all who interact with your organization, including employees, customers, industry, and even the community as a whole.

Companies with healthy cultures ooze value. Innovation thrives. Customer loyalty and satisfaction are superior. Employee and customer retention is high. Company financials are predictable and sustainable. Stakeholders take pride in their accomplishments. Shareholders invest because it is profitable.

Internally, effective strategies and tactics shape culture to achieve its potential. Production, R&D, supply chain, administration, marketing, and sales all contribute to culture. Every department and employee is a cultural contributor. With positive culture, enterprise capacity accelerates and expands because the enterprise talent pool is capable of capitalizing on new opportunities.

Management, employees, and shareholders all thrive with a quality culture. Sound too good to be true. Well, it's not. Nearly every industry has one or two dominant players who have exactly this scenario in place.

From the Employee's View: Cultural Health

What is it like to be an employee of your company?

You know your organization, but every member of your team may experience your company culture differently. To determine what it is like, I suggest you thoroughly consider the answers to the following health-check questions:

- Are vision, mission, and core values really integrated into the company's daily business practices?
- Are strategies and tactics well planned and executed?
- Do tactics create value or merely activity?
- Is the management team transformational and communicative?
- Is the company work environment positive or toxic?
- Do business ethics and professionalism stand firm against harassment and discrimination?

Employee Retention

Employee retention communicates a great deal about the culture of the company.

In your organization, is management a revolving door of new faces? How many new hires actually survive the first year or two?

There is something to be said for organizations who bring in new ideas and people to revolutionize. However, it is a very different scenario when you continually lose your employees and have to replace them.

For one, hiring new employees is an expensive investment. You invest time and money to bring on someone new, let alone to get them established in your company.

Additionally, when they leave, what are they taking with them? Is it the relationships with clients they have built while wearing your company hat? Because that lost relationship could directly affect company the company bottom line substantially more than just one lost hire.

Another aspect of retention is mentorship. Ask yourself, is facilitating subordinate success, training, and leadership a management priority in your company? Are you truly investing in the growth of your employees?

Communication

Employees are cultural ambassadors to customers and vendors. It is commonly believed that

- 55% of communication is body language
- 38% is the tone of voice
- 7% is the actual words spoken.

With that in mind, what message do your employees communicate to the customer? While your organization might have a sales script or other avenue to streamline communication, that potentially leaves 93% of what employees are saying up for interpretation. Your clients are smart; they can tell if the employee believes the words they say.

Management shapes the cultural environment, while employees live it and communicate it. Culture is transparent and has few secrets. Customers, vendors, and community establish perception about the organization.

Tip: 360° Organizational Assessments provide great insight and metrics into better understanding and modifying company culture.

From the Customer's View: Cultural Health

What's it like to be a customer of your company?

Customers are not just purchasing products; they are purchasing the company brand with every order. They have a laundry list of expectations: quality, service, value, relationship, and innovation, among others.

Achieving customer expectations demonstrates the health of company culture. We suggest the vast majority of soured customer relationships are not based on price, but rather dysfunctional business practices and relationships.

Ask yourself these questions about your organization:

- Are quality, service, and value consistent and predictable?
- Is innovation truly innovative?
- Are both customer loyalty and satisfaction measured and verified?
- Does top management have a one-to-one relationship with key customers?
- Do customers consider your company to be the premier supplier and innovator?

Key customer surveys are a real wake-up call for determining the facts regarding company culture. When it's discovered a company's top volume accounts are not enamored with the relationship, quality, or service, it's time to address the challenges.

The fact is that quality customers have clear expectations. Flawed cultures diminish the value of products and innovation. Customers with bad experiences simply find other more qualified suppliers.

Tip: 360 Customer Surveys measure customer satisfaction and provide insight into better understanding customer loyalty and expectations.

Strategy and Tactics: The Combination of Success

First, let us differentiate strategy and tactics.

- Strategy is a carefully devised plan of action to achieve a goal.
- Tactics are the actions and activities necessary to achieve the strategy.

An effective strategy plots a course of success for the organization. It defines a climate for critical thinking and self-management. Effective tactics achieve the strategy efficiently. Efficient tactics focus the enterprise on activities with the greatest return on investment.

Organizations with effective strategies and tactics are constantly vetting and refining the approach to achieve competitive advantage. In our view, every company department should have a clear strategy contributing to the goal.

Strategic organizations are objective based. Tactical organizations are activity based. That is, tactical-based companies sometimes fail to consistently achieve objectives.

Strategic organizations generally demonstrate a high-performance culture. In a strategic organization everyone understands the company course and is committed to its success. Interestingly, we often find enterprises that are labeled strategic are, in reality, tactical.

Consider this:

> "Strategy without tactics is the slowest route to victory. Tactics without strategy is the noise before defeat." — Sun Tzu, The Art of War.

Ask yourself:

- What strategies does your organization have in place to keep a positive organizational culture?
- What tactics are planned to achieve that strategic goal?

- How are those tactics measured for their own success?
- What is the process for brainstorming or implementing new tactics?
- How would you approach changing tactics while keeping true to the overall strategy?

Is Cultural Health a Priority for Your Brand?

What do you want your company culture to broadcast?

Companies with fast and sustainable growth are highly aware of culture. It's the source of competitive advantage. Employees demonstrate it in their job descriptions. Customers feel it in every communication and order placed.

As an example, look at how Amazon has reshaped the retail sales environment through its business model. The organization has come a long way from book sales; it has driven online e-commerce to explode, and in doing so, it's completely changed the way we shop.

Even externally, other brick-and-mortar stores have been immensely impacted by "The Amazon Effect" (Source Forbes)

As written by Amazon CEO Jeff Bezos in his 2016 annual letter, "...customers want something better, and your desire to delight customers will drive you to invent on their behalf... [Success] requires you to experiment patiently, accept failures, plant seeds, protect saplings, and double down when you see customer delight." (Source Business Insider)

Quality customers realize flawed supplier cultures cost them financially and emotionally. There is simply not enough profit margin in business today to purchase from suppliers with challenged cultures. Again, customers are buying your brand and not just the products.

It's estimated as the boomer generation retires, x-y generations, millennials, and foreign workers will comprise approximately 60% of the U.S. workforce. Never before has critical thinking, effective communication, and work environment been so important. Doubting, just ask them about the value of culture.

Employee retention, given the low unemployment rate of today, is critical. If a business culture is flawed, skilled and quality employees generally move to a better environment.

Culture, strategy, and tactics establish brand perception. Both workforce and customer expectations have evolved. Those enterprises embracing change best deliver competitive advantage.

Tip: Interview your most important customers personally for real truth about company performance. Find any ideas that customers have that could positively impact the relationship.

Solution: Sustainable Change

Change solutions begin first with measuring and understanding the cultural health of the enterprise. You are unable to create a positive, effective culture if you don't know your specific starting point and the challenges associated with it.

Once your management team understands the cultural health of your organization, then a developmental plan must be crafted to modify culture, strategy, and tactics. Then your organization, from the top executives to the newest hires, must all work together with open communication to follow that crafted, strategic plan.

We know from experience in most cases, rapid change causes both customers and employees to distrust the brand. It's simply human nature. Alternatively, steady and consistent change is sustainable.

Tip: 360 Organizational Assessment and Customer Surveys provide factual evidence to management teams in order to revolutionize cultural change.

Revolutionize

If your company lacks critical thinking, effective communication, and clear strategy, then you must revolutionize. When business practices, tactics, and innovation are challenged, you must choose to revolutionize.

Otherwise, customers will adjust your employees and market share accordingly.

As an exercise, we suggest you go section through section of this Article to critically consider each of the questions asked. Talk with your team members in other areas of the organization to determine other perspectives. How does your organization compare? What are the points that have room for improvement?

Businesses today are constantly changing. As such, you must consider your company culture to be fluid, changing every day with every interaction internally and externally.

In a perfect world, that culture would stay true to your organizational strategy. However, conversely, it can also change quickly when individuals in the company do not follow the company cultural strategy.

We suggest periodic health checks to investigate the success of your revolutionized culture. If you find pain points, you can then be proactive in eradicating them.

Concepts to Ponder

1. In reality, is your culture really your brand?
2. What is your definition of company culture?
3. What would your customers say about your company culture?

Article 25
Selecting Quality Employees

Selecting quality employees is a challenge for many businesses. Unemployment is low, complicating the efforts to staff key positions. However, before you leap to hire a new employee, why did the last employee leave?

In some cases, an employee departure was mutual, or suggested. In other situations, the business lost a quality employee for unknown reasons. As a side note, the business also lost a valuable employee investment.

When management terminates an employee for performance or behavior, the reasons are clear. The employee was not fulfilling their job description or had demonstrated unprofessional behavior.

When the business loses a quality employee who has fulfilled their job description and demonstrated professional behavior, management should pause and take note. There are probably indications other behaviors and practices going on.

While some quality employees leave because of compensation and benefits, many leave over existing business practices. Often times, the story senior management receives are compensation was the reason for termination when the truth is much different.

Challenged business practices alienate quality employees. They decide to seek new employment when the business consistently oversteps their personal boundaries. The business forces the employee to seek other opportunities.

These are several more notable business practices resulting in employee attrition we have observed.

Job Descriptions

Poorly defined and measured job descriptions complicate the manager and employee relationship. Employees want to know the specific requirement of their job. When employees fail to receive these structural job expectations, they feel overworked. They feel they are being mistreated.

Effective and well-written job descriptions also identify for management key requirements and attributes necessary for a new hire.

Equal Accountability

Employees should be held equally accountable for performance. Management favoritism and personal relationships deliver disastrous consequences. The bar of excellence declines as poor and superior performers are equally rewarded by management. Employees view unequal accountability as a direct insult.

Opportunity

Not everyone wants advancement into management. However, most quality employees want opportunities to improve themselves. These improvements can come in many forms. Education, new skills, technology, different departmental jobs, and employee team leaders are just a few ideas. The fact is these opportunities do not need to be expensive; they can be scalable to your business.

On Boarding

On boarding is not training. On Boarding is a structured setting where management communicates information and expectations about history, culture, business practices, and customers. The process discusses quality and its relationship to company products and services.

It's also the time to review the employee handbook and clearly establish communication expectations and behavioral boundaries of the organization. Transparency builds trust and loyalty.

On Boarding is the time for the company to be very clear in its responsibilities to employees and management to "Walk the Talk." The moment the company fails to achieve their employee responsibilities, they set the stage for employee attrition.

Training

Superior organizations are focused on continuous education. Education expands the mind and offers the employee opportunities for growth. Education is a proactive approach to reducing stagnation.

In addition, training isn't just about learning new skills; it's also an opportunity for management to connect with employees. Training sessions are a great time for refresher courses on company culture and innovation.

Management

Some managers are facilitators and transformational in approach. They create a work environment where employees are happy, communicative, and productive. These managers offer predictable style and leadership. Employee respect and loyalty are high with this quality of manager.

Customers have the same experience with transformational managers. They know when there are product or service challenges this manager will address their individual needs. Customer loyalty and satisfaction are constantly cultivated and measured. Employees are not exposed nearly as often to irate customers when management is proactive and involved in the business.

Challenged management teams are generally reactive in approach. For challenged managers replacing employees is standard operating procedure rather than examining the real reasons why employees leave.

Employee Retention

Employee retention speaks volumes about the organization to employees, customers, and community. Often times, our best opportunities for selecting and retaining quality employees come from within the organization.

What's interesting about quality companies is they need to recruit and select fewer employees. They can focus on quality rather than quantity. In the community, they are known for being a quality organization. Current employees spread the word about their success. They are ambassadors of the company.

I mentioned earlier that employees are a financial investment. When we retain skilled and productive employee's company value increases to the customer. Customer surveys frequently report high turnover is a concern to them from suppliers. It's a systemic risk by the supplier to the customer.

Quality employees simply build better interpersonal relationships with customers. Customers expect consistency. They want to know their challenges and opportunities are being addressed.

Quality Management

So, before you select a new employee, assess your business practices. It may be your wages are low prompting employee attrition. Nevertheless, I suggest for many enterprises, its business practices contribute not only to employee attrition, but to customer attrition as well.

When compensation and benefits are the only binding relationship to employees, your business becomes irrelevant. Relevant businesses are delivering best practices, fair compensation and benefits, and leadership.

Be honest, direct, and fair as you assess the truth about your business. Seek to recruit, select, and retain quality employees.

Concepts to Ponder

1. Does your organization have a candidate selection process?

2. Does the company utilize performance directed job descriptions?
3. Does the company training process achieve its objectives?

Article 26

Boiled Business (Frog) Syndrome

The "Boiled Business (Frog) Syndrome" creates Gatekeepers. These gatekeepers not only limit company and personal success, but they also drain company resources. Circumstances and events manage the business rather than opportunity.

Let's first remember the original fable. It goes like this:

"A frog is slowly being boiled alive. If a frog is put suddenly into boiling water, it will jump out. But, if the frog is put in tepid water which is then slowly brought to a boil, it will not perceive the danger and will be cooked to death."

For the purpose of this Article, now consider a business-related version of that fable:

"When the business is put in the tepid waters of ineffective leadership, communication, and poor perception, which is then brought to a boil slowly over time, it will not perceive the danger. Slowly, the business will be cooked to death."

No industry is immune to this syndrome. Some people incorrectly believe that large companies have solved these challenges with their layers of strategists and management.

Ask Volkswagen, Wells Fargo, or the many challenged retailers. Businesses that fail to manage changing culture and customer satisfaction are simply boiling to death while prioritizing, engaging, and reacting to the wrong indicators.

Throughout this paper, we introduce questions that you must honestly ask yourself to determine the true state of your organization. Often when a company encounters difficulty, some of that problem can be traced back to leadership, communication, perception, and most importantly, culture.

As you read this Article, please let go the distractions of business mechanics. This includes technology, CRM, ERP, market intelligence, production equipment, and distribution. Consider every question honestly, both as an employee of your company, and as a leader of your organization.

By having an accurate picture of the current state of culture, your organization can be proactive in ensuring that your team keeps true to organizational values, and in turn, keeps from boiling to death.

Leadership

Successful organizations look at leadership vertically. That is; owners, senior management, and secondary management are first responsible for enforcing cultural expectations equally and fairly.

Each are responsible for communicating, executing, and verifying that company core values, quality, perception, and business practices are aligned and communicated to the customer with each transaction.

Transformational leaders achieve more objectives because they place culture and perception as a first priority. They are transformational leaders because they are constantly in tune with both customers and employees.

"Your Culture is Your Brand" is more than a simple statement. When company core values and statements are not enforced, it is a sign that company business practices are out of alignment.

While price is the issue in some transactions, poor business relationships and practices also have a large impact on customer retention. Customers who feel slighted go elsewhere and the company loses a valuable revenue source.

When companies effectively manage culture and core values, customer satisfaction is generally high. Satisfied customers are usually loyal customers. Loyal customers are more collaborative and receptive to innovation. Unhappy and dissatisfied customers choose not to invest further with suppliers demonstrating poor business practices.

Core Values

- Do customer satisfaction results accurately reflect your company core values?
- Does management consistently "walk the talk" of vision, mission, and core values to the team and customers?

Tip: Identify managers with excessive employee attrition rates, or those with none at all. Assess how these managers compare with the expectations of your top managerial talent.

Brand Perception

Brand perception is viral and directly contributes to the boiling temperature. Perception starts at the top of the management chain and trickles down to the bottom of the organization. From there, employees spread perception in every communication and transaction of the company.

There are really few secrets in business, we just think so. Positive perception establishes employee trust. Positive customer perception leads to consistent purchase orders and customer satisfaction. Customer satisfaction leads to customer retention.

Employees are ambassadors of perception. Positive employee perception achieves more objectives. It's also an open invitation to new candidates about joining the right team.

Tacticware provides 360° Organizational Assessments to our clients. Interestingly from our client experiences, two common challenges are most discussed by employees:

- Equal Accountability: Where departmental managers fail to equally and fairly enforce quality and performance standards. Eventually the bar of excellence is set by the weakest employee.

- Management Communication: Where management communication of company status, meetings, objectives, challenges, innovation, and achievement is poorly executed, inconsistent, or disappointing.

Generally, activity-based management results in unequal accountability and poor communication. Objective-based management is generally proactive and facilitates equal accountability and communication while supporting a quality work environment.

Questions

- What are the customer attrition rates for your organization?
- What are the employee attrition rates for your organization?

Strategic Planning

Strategic planning is influenced by culture and leadership. Companies with flawed strategies communicate a message to both employees and customers. The effects of the Boiling Syndrome are increased when plans are flawed or poorly conceived.

> *Customers view flawed strategy as an absence of leadership.*

Customers view flawed strategy as an absence of leadership and sometimes as a lack of customer understanding and market conditions. Customer trust flies out the door when poor planning occurs because customers begin to question supplier trust and value.

Some companies have invested vast financial resources pursuing flawed strategies. Eventually these flawed strategies became toxic strategies. A few toxic strategies can pour gasoline into the boiling cauldron.

Quality and high-performance employees view flawed strategy as a reason to look for another job. Why risk working for an organization that is self-defeating? With unemployment at less than 3% in many markets, good people can and will secure another job.

Strategic planning is an extension of company core values.

Strategic thinking is a process and is more often about what "we should not do, rather than how to do it."

Transformational leaders separate strategy and tactics from the discussion. They accurately assess company risk and strategic contribution to company growth.

Company Capacity

Consider this, Company Capacity is generally limited to its Management's Capacity. Strategic plans exceeding company resources or tactics often lead to failed execution.

Who is at fault when strategy fails? Generally, management blames employees and employees blame management. Employees feel unrealistic objectives are the cause and management feels unqualified employees are the cause. The final result is the strategy failed and contributed to the "Boiled Business Syndrome."

The Five Greats of Customer Satisfaction

Consider your last significant strategic plan. Were company core values, brand perception, and customer satisfaction included as discussion points and risk management concerns?

Customers consistently expect the Five Greats. The question is how many managers and strategic plans effectively engage these qualities. The result is competitive advantage.

The Five Greats

1. <u>Quality</u>: products/service are exactly as promised
2. <u>Relationships</u>: consistent relationships that are professional and timely
3. <u>Service</u>: consistent and friendly solutions resolving challenges
4. <u>Innovation</u>: that is truly innovative and relevant
5. <u>Value</u>: fair and predictable pricing

Quality

Quality companies are predictable. The term "Quality" applies to the entire organization's management, employees, products, and distribution network. Customers know they can depend on the company to correct any deficiency.

Relationships

Professional and timely relationships create customer trust and collaboration. Customer relationships are not just the responsibility of sales; every company employee and department is responsible.

Service

Customers expect friendly solutions from supportive staff who actually care. Positive resolution of challenges set the tone for a future transaction. Satisfied customers generally are loyal customers.

Innovation

Effective innovation is the source of new revenue and an opportunity to renew collaborative relationships with the customer. Unhappy customers with sore feelings about prior quality complaints or lack of relationship simply are not the right candidates for innovation. Customers with positive perception are statistically more likely to purchase innovation because of previously established trust.

Value

Quality customers expect suppliers to charge a fair price for products and services. Quality, service, and innovation have a price, and this creates value.

Commodity-driven customers sometimes fail to value a quality organization. If your company has a number of significant customers falling into the commodity category, consider the type of customers your sales team is soliciting and why.

(Notice that Value/Price are #5. If the conditions of Quality, Relationship, Service, and Innovation are achieved, the condition of Price is less important.)

More often than not, customers leave suppliers because of poor business practices and perception, rather than price. What's important for management to know is which scenario really happened.

A Profound Question

If we were to measure and benchmark each of the "Five Greats" for your organization, what would be the result?

Tip: Interview your most important customers personally for real truth about company performance. Find any ideas that customers have that could positively impact the relationship.

The ability of a business to adapt and prosper when confronted by adversity, competitors, and market conditions is the highest level of risk management. Effective leadership, communication, and positive perception is the foundation of customer satisfaction.

Concepts to Ponder

1. Is your company boiling in a pot of chaos?
2. What methods is your company utilizing to limit gatekeepers?
3. How does your organization deliver the Five Greats?

Summary

Successful leaders surround themselves with other successful leaders. As a management team, each share common values, ethics, and passion.

Without leadership and effective communication, the business stagnates. Without strong culture, employee and customer relationships fail to thrive. Without strategy, the destination is obscure.

If your organization is challenged, assess the facts and evidence. Identify the source, not the symptoms. And if your situation warrants, contact me to assist in your transformation.

Thank you for reading.

Paul R. Fournier

www.ingramcontent.com/pod-product-compliance
Lightning Source LLC
Chambersburg PA
CBHW071043240526
45471CB00014B/339